My Daddy Fought the Cold War

Not Entirely Serious Tales of a Foreign Service Career

As Recalled/Claimed/Professed By

C. Robert (Bob) Dickerman
Working Stiff/Diplomat Emeritus

Copyright © 2011 by C. Robert (Bob) Dickerman.

ISBN 978-1-4507-8346-0

Website: www.MyDaddyFoughtTheColdWar.com

This book was printed in the United States of America.

For large quantities or author inquiries, contact AFP Publishing:
P.O. Box 1193, Waynesboro, Va. 22980
(540) 949-6574 | www.afpbusiness.com

FOR DAVID + SHEILA

AN UNORTHODOX
memoir

NOW DO YOURS!

Boo
2/2012

Dedication

~ for daughters Julia and Anneke ~

In the Spring of 1991,
some 18 months after the imploding of the
Berlin Wall,
we took the girls from Copenhagen to Berlin.
We went to the Brandenburg Gate, from both ends of which,
since 1961, the infamous Berlin Wall had divided East and West,
both locally and globally.
I had last seen the Wall in mid-1963, when it was newly-built,
and both lower and less lethal than it was to become.
I had then just concluded my first year abroad as a
Foreign Service Officer.
Since I would retire in 1992, my career spanned the duration
of this grim symbol of what the "Cold War" was all about.

I tried to tell the girls, then 8 and 10, about the Wall.
They looked both north and south.

They saw only manicured grass and bike and walking trails.
"Let's get ice cream," one said.

They would live in a different world.
But this is some of their Dad's story.

Acknowledgements

So many people to thank:
- Daughters Julia and Anneke, of course: for giving purpose to this, as to so many other endeavors.
- Five old (and not getting any younger!) Antioch College classmates who encouraged putting these tales into print: Gordon Munro, Warren McKay, Edward Bing, Robert Yuan and John Gunning. Very especial thanks as well to Gordon's wife Teresa, dubbed this book's "honorary illustrator."
- Four lovely ladies who not only encouraged this but proofread and corrected it, and even admitted to having "occasionally laughed out loud" when doing so: sister Marianne Dickerman Caldwell, Charlottesville librarian Watts Schwab, and former wives (and still, happily, "best friends") Christina Lundblom Dickerman and Gerhild Sachs Dickerman.
- Crystal Abbe Graham, co-owner of Augusta Free Press Publishing L.L.C. in Waynesboro, Virginia, without whose formatting skills and publishing know-how this venture would have been impossible.
- The friends, colleagues and family members who through the decades shared in these adventures, or, more commonly, endured hearing of them (perhaps repeatedly?).And of these: especial thanks to two individuals who, justifiably or not, made possible two of the most rewarding challenges of my professional life: Professor Joseph S. Nye, Jr., of Harvard University, and Ambassador Sheldon J. Krys.

The responsibility for any errors or failings herein is, of course, my own.

Table of Contents

Explaining Vietnam II
I'm So Sorry, General Park
Direct from the Lunar Landing (Almost)
My Windowette to Norway
Grass Roots: New and Ancient
The Inspectors
Off to Harvard

Harvard? Me??!, 1970-71, 1972-73
pages 159 - 165

Getting There
The Kennedy School Year
An "Opportunity of a Lifetime," Botched?
A Correlation
Matchmaker

Iceland, 1973-75
pages 166 - 182

A Complexity of Memories
Introduction to Iceland
Innocents Abroad
The Fish; the Base
"No Lefties....."
Vic I
Vic II
Vic III
Liberating Our Troops One Woman at a Time
Oddities (Charms!)
The Fun Side of Watergate
Sami Sense
My Window to Iceland: Frank Ponzi

Denmark, 1990-92

Foreword

A Reasonably Genial Curmudgeon

A reasonably genial curmudgeon sits in the cluttered living room of his 80-year-old Appalachian farm house. The place has not benefited from the presence of a resident female for some 35 years. A falling down pre-Civil War barn is outside the south window; a creek, a pond, a mountain and a mountain roadway are to the east. Most of the farm's 98 acres are to the west, sloping upward through the George Washington National Forest toward Eliot's Knob, the highest point in Virginia north of the James River.

The septuagenarian was born just ten miles from here, in the midst of the Great Depression. Quite a number of folks here in western Augusta County could say the same. But there are probably few here who have wandered quite as far, or been influenced by quite as many people, places and experiences. Thus the self-described "geezer" has to be careful, in much company, lest his interlocutors dissolve discretely into the company of others, wondering how old IS this guy, anyway?:

"While Reggy and Erik loaded the wagon, I drove the team ....

"When the iceman and his horse brought the day's block to the front door ...."

"The 'colored' and 'white' toilets, drinking fountains and waiting rooms ....

"The Pullman car from Elyria, Ohio, to Staunton, Virginia ...

"The Underwood typewriter ....

"The Kungsholm, the ocean liner we took to Europe ....

"The nickel admission to the ice rink; the nickel newspaper; the three cent stamp; the penny postcard ....

"The Nash, the Studebaker, the Hudson, the Packard ....

"In Vietnam ....

"In Chicago ....

"In Somalia ....

"In Columbus ....

"In Iceland ... Barbados ... Trinidad ... Denmark ... Norway ... Finland ... Germany.

"In Oberlin, Bloomington, Battle Creek and Arlington ...

"Working the assembly line in Düsseldorf ...

"In the Washington bureau of the Associated Press ...

"My Swedish mother-in-law ...

"My German mother-in-law ...

"Running our Embassy in Trinidad ...

"Running our Cultural Center in Iceland ...

"The Astronauts ...

"Congress ...

"The farming ...

"The log cabin on Dry Branch ...

"The $100 first car (used); the $2,950 first new car (the Volvo) ...

"Driving dump truck in Ohio ...

"Our chauffeur in Trinidad ...

"My black pajamas in Vietnam; my black tie in Norway ...

"The weddings in Harvard Yard, Buffalo Gap and Waikiki ...

"Harvard ...

"Buffalo Gap ...

"Dad's Model A Ford."

And much else which, when dropped unthinkingly, aligns me with — if not weirdos — then, at the least, with folks that "sure ain't like us":

"The nice family dinner at the President's home in Trinidad ..."

"The ostriches that we chased on the Vespas ..."

"Those temple carvings in Katmandu ..."

"Serengeti ..."

"The hot springs in northern Iceland ..."

"Martha Graham asked me to ..."

So perhaps I should explain. Move away, if you like. Otherwise: read on.

Introduction

Too Far Away from Everything

I've lived in quite a few places that folks never heard of. I'd never heard of some of them either, before being told that such-and-such would be my home for the next two or three years. I would then arrive there, knowing no one ... and eventually come to feel that it was the very center of the world. There was loneliness at first, of course, and objectively seen, some of these places were really strange, and off the beaten track, and even, perhaps, fully deserving of the obscurity in which they existed ...and continue to exist. But I had heard a story soon after arriving at my first Foreign Service post, Helsinki, Finland, which seemed, at each successive post, to fit my own experience.

Apparently the city of Helsinki had celebrated, a few months before my arrival in April, 1962, a great anniversary of its founding. Perhaps it was the city's 1,000[th] birthday.

In any case, there was a week of celebrations, to which notables and dignitaries from throughout Finland, Scandinavia, Europe and the world were invited. Among them was a white-haired Lapp fogda, a Sami chieftain from a nomadic, reindeer-herding family in northernmost Finnish Lapland. He had not, I was told, even been to the capital of Lapland, Rovaniemi, until going to that city's airport en route to the festivities in Helsinki.

He was in Helsinki through the week, and appeared to enjoy himself immensely (although it is said that it is sometimes a bit hard to tell with a Lapp, since they are supposedly even less expressive than the

Finns). In any case, he was interviewed by a reporter from Finnish Radio while awaiting the plane that would fly him back north.

"How was the week?" asked the reporter.

"Not bad," said the chieftain.

"How were the festivities?"

"Not bad."

"And the food?"

"Not bad."

"And the drinks?"

"Not bad."

"And the women?"

"Not bad."

"And the city itself?"

"Not bad."

"So would you like to live here?" asked the reporter.

"NO!," he answered emphatically.

"But why not?"

"Too far away from everything," he replied.

And thus, through the years, did places including My Tho, Vietnam; Mogadishu, Somalia; Reykjavík, Iceland; Bridgewater, Barbados, and Port-of-Spain, Trinidad, and Arlington and Buffalo Gap, Virginia, become the centers of my world .... with everything else, during those years, "too far away from everything." I remember my frustration, for example, while vacationing in Europe one summer, at not being able to find any news of what was going on in Grenada, St. Vincent, St. Lucia, Antigua, Dominica or St. Kitts/Nevis — countries with which, while working in Barbados, I was following daily.

Every place, my friends, is someone's center of the world. And everywhere else, is simply "too far away from everything."

Finland, 1957, 1962-63

"The Crazy American"

I'd been in Denmark, where I'd be spending the 1957-58 academic year, only a week or so when I read that there was to be, shortly, an international conference of the "student press" in Helsinki.

"Well, I've been a journalist," I said. "And I'm an American student. And I've at least hung around the Antioch College newspaper's office. And I'm almost there!"

So I wrote a letter to the National Student Association (NSA) in, I believe, Philadelphia. "If you'll pay my ticket, I'll gladly represent you/us there."

A letter promptly came back designating me as the NSA's delegate to the conference. A check for $100 was enclosed. I took the train from Copenhagen, crossing the Øresund from Denmark to Sweden at Helsingør, and continuing on to Stockholm.

The Øresund is only four kms wide between Helsingør and, on the Swedish side, Helsingborg. Ferries, for both cars and trains, shuttled back and forth continually.

I was to be in Helsinki the next morning. I wandered around Stockholm for a bit (little imagining that that beautiful city would later become my "city-in-law"), and then decided that I might as well get over to Helsinki this same afternoon. So I found the pier from which the Helsinki ship was soon to sail, bought my ticket, and went on board. Another essential geography lesson for the Innocent Abroad: the distance from Stockholm to Helsinki is 417 kms, not four, as between Helsingør and Helsingborg; the voyage is an overnight trip, and had I missed that ship there would not have been another until the following day.

But if the Swedish-Finnish voyage had worked out serendipitously, the same could not be said for the impression that I was going to make at the "International Student Press Conference" on the campus of the Finnish Technical Institute.

I was, first of all, at 20, the youngest "delegate" there. I was, in fact, an actual current student. My fellow delegates from the Western European countries were, at least temporarily, full time student politicians, and in their late 20's. And the delegates from three of the four Communist countries — the Soviet Union, Yugoslavia and Czechoslovakia — were in their mid-40's, at least. They were, in the tradition of heavy-handed totalitarian diplomacy, professional "student" bureaucrats.

Not only was I the youngest but, because the conference seating was alphabetical, I was seated beside these heavy-jowled Soviet and Yugoslav characters.

No one had briefed me; I had absolutely zero experience in international student politics, or international politics in general. The other delegates were all old hands at these conferences. And when I cast my first vote, there was consternation:

This was 1957; well into the Cold War. Everything was divided: NATO in the West, the Warsaw Pact in the East; the Hague-based International Student Conference (ICS) in the West; the Prague-based International Union of Students (IUS) in the East.

But what did Bob Dickerman, boy liberal from the lefty Antioch College, know about this???? I knew that there should, in theory, be better "communication" and "understanding" between the peoples, and of course between the students of the Communist and the non-Communist worlds. I recalled that our then-President, Dwight D. Eisenhower, had advocated "open skies," and "people-to-people" programs, and "international understanding."

So when the Soviet and Yugoslav gents seated next to me put forth and seconded a motion to exchange, between the student organizations of the East and West, the respective publications of the ICS and the IUS, I voted "yes."

The astonishment and concern that this vote caused among the

Scandinavian, German, British, Dutch, Swiss, Canadian and French delegates was palpable. I think the session was even adjourned for a while.

It was evidently established practice in the Cold War-driven (and financed) international student politics of the time that the U.S. representative(s) was/were indeed the "leader of the free world."

There followed a couple of other votes on which I was evidently out of line. The Western/ISC position was that the IUS was a fraud; that it did not represent students at all; that it was an instrument of Soviet Bloc foreign policy.

During the breaks I was quizzed persistently by my Western "allies." Did I know so and so forth? What had I done with the (U.S.) National Student Association? What preparation for this had I had?

It took them some time — and a one-on-one lunch with Regula Steiner, the Swiss delegate and the heartthrob of the conference — for my Western friends to conclude that: (1) I didn't know a damned thing about what was going on; (2) how I came to represent the US here was incomprehensible, and (3) I was, in Regula's term, "this crazy American." I was from that point on forgiven and, in our plenary sessions, ignored.

Following the two-day conference, we were piled into a bus for a Finnish Student Union-hosted tour of Finland's lake district. We also drove to the Finnish-Soviet border where, all (except the Communists) agreed, the contrast on each side of the wooded demarcation line was every bit as significant as those in much-contested Berlin.

I remember an evening "piss stop" along a wooded road: "ladies to the left, gents to the right." These stops were not infrequent since large quantities of Finnish beer were being consumed en route. At one point it was realized that we seemed to have left the two Poles behind. They had kept their distance from the Soviet and Yugoslav apparatchiks, and had even indicated their envy of the Finns, "who were just damned lucky to keep their freedom after the war while we lost ours."

The bus driver — by now the only sober person aboard — turned back, and we eventually found our Polish friends, walking along the darkening road. "Our only fear," they told us, "was that we might be headed East, not West."

I thus returned to Denmark a wiser individual in spite of this first fiasco in endeavoring to represent my country abroad. We who had been in high school and college during the scourge of McCarthyism would be forever after wary of "anti-communist" rhetoric. It was important, then, that I learn, in Scandinavia, that (1) Poles, Hungarians, East Germans and others ruled by Communist dictatorships did, indeed, yearn for the liberties and democracy that we took for granted; (2) that "Communist Front" organizations were, in fact, real, cynical, exploitative and manipulated by goons; and (3) that many of the individuals and organizations who were fighting the day-to-day struggles with anti-democratic forces, whether on factory floors, in unions halls, in political parties or in Central Europe and the Baltic, actually did rely upon, and need, responsible "American leadership."

But whether it was "responsible" for the Central Intelligence Agency, as was revealed in 1967, to "indirectly" fund the ISC and to recruit student representatives from the United States National Student Association, is of course debatable.

On the other hand: if my lackadaisical selection to represent the NSA at this ICS conference was in any way typical, then what is one to think of such CIA endeavors at all?

What they in fact actually did, as other recollections here will relate, was to forever smear the reputations and integrity of very many, very decent, very committed, and often very idealistic fighters of the Cold War's ideological trench warfare — few if any of whom had any idea where portions of their funding was coming from.

Like the Swiss beauty Regula Steiner. Like others who were so perplexed by what "this crazy American" was up to at this international student press conference.

Wrong Footed, Again

But before we leave Finland's beautiful lake district, one more heart-wrenching tale:

As is well known, dancing is as beloved in Finland as are hard spirits. The two are often mixed quite memorably, but here we're focusing on dancing.

I'm a horrible dancer. Can hardly do the box step taught in high school PE. In other countries, at least, a stray bachelor, even if coordinately challenged, might await a "slow dance," and meet a female interlocutor nevertheless.

But in Finland, the bar was much higher. One (two, actually!) had to do THREE dances together: and they would be three different kinds: MAYBE a "slow dance," and almost certainly a waltz ... but then a tango (!), rumba (!), jitterbug or such.

Another part of the boy-meets-girl protocol, at least in the age group I was interested in, was that (1) unless dancing the boys stood on one side of the floor, the girls on the other; (2) at the first note of the next three-dance series, the boys would rush over to the girls' side, grab the one they most desired, and (3) haul her out onto the floor.

These "couples" then usually danced diligently enough but seemed rarely to look one another in the eye (either could grope, apparently, but not gaze). Instantaneously, when the third number in the set ended, each would hasten back to his/her side.

Unless, sometime during the dance, a rendezvous outside or afterwards had been agreed to.

We were camping in tents each night as our beer-laden International Student Press Conference bus proceeded through beautiful southeastern Finland. On a Saturday evening we checked into a camping area along a particularly gorgeous lake. (The characteristic landscape of Finland — the one you must always have in mind when listening to Sibelius — is clear blue sky and clear blue water, broken only by a thin horizontal line of fir trees on the opposite shore.)

We supped, imbibed, and headed to the dancing barge. Thereon, as expected, were the randy lads on one side and the perhaps equally desirous lasses on the other. When the music began, the lads rushed over to grab the gal of their desires ... making the whole barge tilt dangerously to its distaff side.

One lovely long-tressed blonde in a red mini-skirt stood out from all the others, and was the cause of much elbowing, and worse, as her would-be suitors sought to immobilize their competition.

I was in more than one of these targeted mêlées as well, and finally Got Her. Not that it did any good: I danced my usual horrible; I tried to use my Danish-adulterated "Finland's Swedish," and she surely was glad to be rid of me after enduring the whole three-piece marathon of inescapable clumsiness.

I eventually returned to the tent which I was sharing with one of our Finnish hosts, Paavo. But Paavo didn't come home that night.

When he finally showed, fresh from a morning swim and more, I asked him where he'd been.

"Remember that long-haired blonde in a red mini-skirt at the dance last night?" he said.

"Of course," said I sadly.

"Well, I told her I was a visiting American student. We spoke English. She loves to speak English. And she loves Americans. So I've been with her all night," he said.

"Maybe you should have tried that too, Bob?" he said.

But it had absolutely simply not occurred to me. Didn't the advertisements say: "Learn Foreign Languages ... Meet Beautiful Women"?

A Most Serendipitous Start

I was next in Finland five years later, for quite a different experience:

Finns are supposed to be — or at least WERE supposed to be, before their country began making it to the top of all sorts of international quality of life indices — a taciturn folk, reserved to the point of dourness; reticent even with their compatriots, and even more so with foreigners, with outsiders.

As reported above, I had been in Finland for a week or so five years earlier, but that was with an international student group. Our Finnish hosts had been genial enough, but I was now prepared for the stereotypical reserve. ("You can always tell a Finnish extrovert: he's the one focusing on your shoes.")

And I knew that I had been lucky not only to have been sent to Europe for my nine-month training assignment, but to the luscious North. If USIA's personnel department seemed to believe that my Danish would help me along in Finland ... so what?

My flight arrived at Helsinki's airport in the afternoon of April 30, 1962. I was met by my new boss, the amiable Ed Savage, and taken to the Vaakuna Hotel in central Helsinki. I was to take a get-over-the-jet-lag nap. Ed would then return, and I'd have supper at the Savages' home.

But I'd already noticed, when Ed was dropping me off from the airport, that something fun was going on in the streets: people my age, many with white student hats, guys and lovely gals; laughing, drinking, singing and dancing. For a few moments, I followed the fun along the Kaartenkaupunki park toward the harbor. There, jammed around the fountain and statue of the nude Havis Amanda ("mermaid," but this one a shapely biped nevertheless), were hundreds of what seemed to be the most exuberant young people I could imagine. The Havis Amanda was being "capped" ... but I had to have supper with, and make a good impression upon, my new boss.

I remember nothing of that evening's meal with the Savages except that (1) I certainly was trying to make a good impression, and (2) I was also trying, equally hard, to persuade them that I'd had a long, long trans-Atlantic day — and very, very much needed to get back to the hotel, and to bed.

When I was finally released and Ed had driven me back to the Vaakuna, I scurried to my room, changed to something less diplomatic ... and hurried out into Helsinki's by-now electrifyingly hedonistic streets.

That year was, in retrospect — before the assassination of President Kennedy, before Vietnam; before LBJ and Nixon and more assassinations — just about the last during which it was absolutely grand to be, and to be completely unapologetically, a young American in northern Europe. But of course nationality didn't mean anything on that glorious night of Vappu — and every Finn speaks English after a drink or two. We were on the streets, in the parks, holding hands, in the grass, in one another's arms; laughing, dancing, singing, celebrating. Friends made so easily that light-filled, alcohol-fueled spring night remained my friends through my time in Helsinki. And through them, I met many others.

On that first night in Helsinki, I knew nothing about Vappu, and wasn't thinking, either, of its transition the next morning into the First of May/May Day. For all I knew, these new friends carried on like this every weekend. Maybe, in fact, Finland was that Valhalla in which "every night is Saturday night, and Saturday's New Year's Eve"?

But in fact, those crazily fused 24 hours each year are a remarkable mergence of pre-Christian and Christian traditions, and of Marxist and bourgeois political activism:

Spring, and thus fertility, festivals go back to pagan times, of course. In Northern Europe Christianity then absorbed these (or tried to) into Walpurgis Night. Then, in the latter half of the 19th century, national labor movements — and a growing number of countries — designated May 1st at International Workers' Day, or Labor Day.

Finnish politics through the first three decades of the 20th century could hardly have been more complex: there were competing Russian, German and Swedish influences; linguistic conflicts, clashing views of nationalism, independence and government; conflicts between the rising labor movements and the resistance of the "estates," adjustments to the consequences of universal suffrage — and then, in 1917-18, the near-breakdown of all order as Whites and Reds battled throughout the country as the Russian Empire, and thus the Grand Duchy of Finland, was both embroiled in, and a reflection of, the chaos of the end stages of World War I and the turmoil of the struggles and battles for power in Russia.

Some 37,000 Finns died in this civil war. The nation emerged independent, but with its economy and social structure shattered.

The once-unified labor movement split into three bitterly competing factions: moderate Social Democrats and left-wing socialists in Finland, and communists allied with the support of the Bolsheviks and the emerging Soviet Union.

But what does this have to do with the wonderful raucousness of Vappu?

As my new Helsinki friends eventually explained it: although Finland settled uneasily into its newly-independent parliamentary democracy, bitterness remained, especially on the most militant left.

On May Day each year — International Workers Day — these groups could, and did, mobilize thousands in angry, threatening, banner-filled marches through the capital. There was reason to fear, I was told, that these huge May Day demonstrations could easily lead to a coup; an overthrow of Finland's still-fragile democratic and moderate institutions.

University students then were mostly upper class: conservatives. So what happened, I was told, was that the students resurrected the ages-old spring festival of Vappu. The thought was that the turn-out for, and the energy of, the annual May First demonstrations advocating "revolution" would be quite diminished if/when so many had spent the night before carousing, drinking, dancing, singing, and otherwise spiritedly (!) welcoming the return of spring, the sun, and fertility to the North.

And that is why, when I blissfully strolled the streets of central Helsinki that next morning, sleepless and happy, I noted the strangest of May Day marches: some folks clenched-fisted, chanting and absolutely purposeful; others arm-in-arm, weaving unsteadily, still singing the night's songs, and clinging to festive balloons rather than proletarian placards.

But all, in passing, cheered the Havis Amanda. ..who, in her white student cap, nudely smiled benignly over the festivities.

More Education:
The VIII World Festival of Youth and Students
Helsinki 1962

Less than three months later the "VIII World Festival of Youth & Students" — known in most of the West as "The Eighth Communist Youth Festival — came to Helsinki. Rarely, if ever, have I experienced such a perfect combination of personal pleasure, professional satisfaction, and lasting edification.

It turned out, by pure good fortune, that several of the new "friends" whom I had met that first Vappu night were activists in the Finnish National Student Union — the offices of which were just around the corner from our American Cultural Center in central Helsinki. It was thus easy to keep in contact, and to meet others of the same age groups and interests.

My motivation at that point was entirely social. But the Kennedy Administration was pushing its diplomats worldwide to break away from the oldsters who comprised most of their contacts, and to get to know, and befriend, "up and coming leaders."

So there I was, one of only two Foreign Service Officers in the Embassy who was under 35 or so (I was 26) ... and the other (poor fellow) was married.

Several of my elders and seniors in the Embassy tried to follow Washington's instructions, but they simply weren't up to it. "Damn it,

Bob," said one. "I might be able to manage one of these all-nighters per month ... but not two or three each week!"

Embassy Helsinki, like American Embassies around the world, was required in that period to report by cable to Washington each week on the contacts which its diplomats had had with such "up and coming leaders." Before long the only Embassy officer's activities to be reported (with the whole Embassy taking credit for them) were Bob Dickerman's.

And my bosses and elders were so grateful!

"God, Bob, thank you for doing this," said my immediate boss, Ed Savage. "Don't you worry about being here on time in the mornings. We realize how tough this work must be."

But although I eventually turned some of my observations into memoranda, what drove my commitment to this endeavor was, of course, "social" (as in raunch). Helsinki would have been a delightful place for a young bachelor to be in any summer. But that was the summer of the Youth Festival, and it turned out that my friends in the national student union were well into making plans to counter the "Communist Youth Festival."

Seven previous international "Festivals of Youth and Students," sponsored, hosted by and orchestrated by the Moscow-controlled International Student Union and the World Federation of Democrat Youth, had been held since 1947. The first five had been held in Warsaw Pact nations. That in 1959 had been in Vienna. Now, in 1962, it was to be in Helsinki.

Although Moscow exerted more influence over the Austrian and Finnish Governments than it did those of other Western countries, these two were free, sovereign, with open borders and populations committed to broad freedoms and democratic rule. The Festivals' organizers thus knew that they would encounter some opposition at these two locations — but presumably thought the risk manageable, and this better than a behind-the-Iron-Curtain "festival" which was all too obviously a sham.

What the Finnish students, with the encouragement and support of peers and organizations in Scandinavia, West Germany, the Netherlands, the U.S. and elsewhere planned was ingenious. There would be drinking, dances and other activities to lure the Festival delegates from the official/sanctioned programs. There would be a daily newspaper, in multiple languages, to report activities alongside the Festival — and to expose the machinations of its orchestators, and dissent and opposition where this occurred. A large number of "Third World" participants, most of whom were studying at Lumumba University in Moscow and other similarly-focused schools elsewhere in the Warsaw Pact, and virtually all of whom would be traveling on Festival-provided funds, were to be engaged and, when possible, enticed to transfer immediately, without returning, to Western schools and programs. East European students would also be encouraged to defect.

I thought all of this was great fun. And whatever my linguistic challenges and my miserable dancing, being a bachelor with tax-free booze and a spiffy apartment in Lautisaari often made me, at the end of long evenings, a desirable host.

The official theme of the Festival was "Peace and Friendship." But during the night before it opened, on July 28th, placards appeared all over town showing a dove of peace encaged. "Peace and Friendship," it said, "but what about freedom?"

The large East German and Cuban delegations arrived by ship, as did several others. The East German ship, the M/S Völkerfreundshaft, was berthed far out on one of the most distant, most inaccessible (and well-guarded) piers in Helsinki. It's my recollection that the East German "delegation" numbered some 575, all of whom had presumably worked diligently for months if not years to persuade their regime's keepers of their steadfastness and loyalty. This DDR delegation was permitted off the ship only twice: for the opening and the closing parades through the city. But of the some 575 East German youth who had arrived, fewer than 200 returned. The rest had slipped out of the parades, linking up with Finns, Swedes or West Germans who got them to vehicles which would drive them northward and westward around the Bay of Bothnia to Sweden. They could feel safe only when they reached Sweden. (The land border between Swedish Haparanda and Finnish Tornio on the Bay of Bothnia had slacker passport controls than did the southern harbors. There was concern that, given the power which the USSR continued to exert in Finland, the Finnish government would be unable to refuse were it asked to "repatriate" any such would-be defectors.)

I was interested in the Poles and went aboard their very accessible and welcoming small ship in the harbor ... not far from the Havis

Amanda. These Poles were not going to defect. They were quite open about it: they were going home to fight for the same sort of freedoms that the Finns, also bordering the USSR, enjoyed.

The 400 or 500 member delegation of the Peoples Republic of China was another story. They had arrived via a special train traveling across the entire nine time zones of Russia. Those who were opposing the Festival reported that even in the USSR these Chinese youth had been struck by the seemingly greater prosperity which Russians along the Trans-Siberian railroad enjoyed. And Helsinki???? It was reported — how could it have been confirmed? — that the Chinese delegates were told that "all" of the scarce consumer goods in Western Europe had been brought to Helsinki and put into its store windows just to mislead delegations like theirs. A Potemkin village, in effect.

But although I couldn't confirm that story, I did see something that I thought gave it credence: on the last night of the Festival there was a great outdoor get-together in a Helsinki park. Those who were free to mingle and meet did so. But the Chinese, I saw, were enveloped in a tight circle, with the elbows of the individuals on the outer portions interlocked. None of these "youth and students" was going to experience much "friendship" OR "freedom."

It has been interesting to think back on this Festival from the perspective of several decades since. Today young Chinese, many of whose parents have prospered under capitalism (!) roam the world. They study everywhere.

Poles are again free — and in the European Community and NATO. Germany is re-united; the Wall fell; the DDR imploded, as did the Soviet Union itself. Even the Albanians are independent and economically much better off.

Sometime in the late '90's I saw, at the American Film Institute in the Kennedy Center, a Hungarian film about a group of young people who were, in late 1961/early 1962, scheming to convince the Communist officials who would be deciding that they were exactly the type of loyal individuals whom the authorities could risk sending to the Helsinki Festival. They were chosen; they went, and of course they fled to the West. Although my harder-lined colleagues doubtless suspected — even knew — that this was going on, I probably had doubted it. But subsequent events, and this Hungarian film in particular, certainly confirmed it.

Then, during my next assignment, in Somalia, I met a couple of young men who had been invited to Lumumba University by the Russians, and then sent to the Helsinki Festival. They were among the significant number of Africans who were enticed to remain in the West. But for many, things did not work out. Few if any academic or intellectual skills had been required to be invited to Lumumba. And these two, as many others, simply couldn't manage in whatever West European schools they had ended up in.

One more thing needs to be said about the "VIII World Festival of Youth and Students." Since several leaders of the Finnish students' initiatives to undermine the Festival became my close friends (and one became my first fiancée), I am completely certain that they did what they did out of the most worthy type of commitment and idealism.

What a shame it was, then, when it was revealed in the New York Times of February 11, 1967, that "the Central Intelligence Agency had supported a foundation that sent hundreds of Americans to World Youth Festivals in Vienna in 1959 and Helsinki, Finland, in 1962." There had been rumors to this effect before; rumors which put to question the integrity of some of Finland's then most-outstanding "up and coming political leaders." This revelation — this confirmation — was the final nail in the coffin. Some dropped out of political activity completely. Others, including my onetime fiancée and the son of a prominent "conservative" newspaper publisher, spent many of the following years in quite left-wing, neo-Communist organizations.

At the time of the Festival, I had had only two intimations that something like this might be going on. The first was when one of my weekly memoranda about what the Finnish students planned during the Festival rang a huge alarm in the Embassy's "second political section." They had put a high security classification on my unclassified memo, and warned my boss' boss that "Dickerman should NOT know this stuff."

To which my response was: "Know? Every young Finn knows this, so why shouldn't I???"

The second intimation was in something told me by my immediate boss at USIS Helsinki, press attaché Ed Savage. Ed said that the New York Times' Stockholm bureau chief, Verner Wiskari, who was covering the Festival for the paper, "is snooping around suspecting some CIA involvement in the efforts to undermine the Festival."

I had not met her, but I had seen her: a particularly striking

28-year-old American brunette who had shown up a bit before the Festival and seemed to have close rapport with my Finnish friends.

Yes, her name was Gloria Steinem, And after she invited the Times' correspondent to a tête-à-tête lunch, he dropped this line of questioning.

In the same 1967 Times piece which exposed the (indirect!) CIA connection, the seventh paragraph reads as follows:

"Far from being shocked by this involvement, I was happy to find some liberals in government in those days, who were far-sighted and cared enough to get Americans of all political views to the festival," Miss Steinem said.

And she was right. The point had to be made: "Peace and Friendship, but What About Freedom?"

A Cut Above

"I've got a lot more respect for you, Bob, since I learned you were Jewish."

Well. How in the world does one deal with that if one is, in fact, not Jewish????

But I kept getting this comment (what was I supposed to answer????), and the longer I was in Helsinki, the more I heard it.

Finally I realized ... I don't remember how ... what the explanation was. In Helsinki a good deal of social life involved the sauna. I'd enjoyed many, usually with guys & gals separated, but occasionally not. And it really was ... combined with the drinking and the eating and the après ... a terrific way to meet, get to know, and be with people.

So although I'm not aware that I spend much time in saunas or showers examining others' penises, apparently one's does not go unnoticed. And although Finnish boys of my generation apparently weren't routinely circumcised, I was. So I must be ...quite obviously ... Jewish.

But it turned out that, whatever other implications the question had, Jewish was a very, very good thing for a guy to be! The Finnish ladies — or so I was told — firmly believed that Jewish men were better in bed: "it takes them longer."

And in fact, there were apparently cognoscenti — those who really knew what they were doing — who never went bar-hopping in downtown Helsinki without affixing that Star of David to their lapel.

They get more respect that way, you see.

Whatever It Takes: My First K.I.A.

For several years after I retired in 1992, there was rarely a day that some item of the news didn't involve an individual with whom I'd dealt, however briefly, in my peculiar wanderings. It still happens, though less frequently.

Walter Cronkite died in 2009, at age 92. Although he had eventually hosted the 12 part PBS series on Scandinavia!!! for which I had written the basic treatment, what NPR's tribute to him reminded me of, instead, was the first person that I had killed in the line of duty. My first K.I.A. as it were.

In the NPR story, Mr. Cronkite was recalling his anchoring of the very first trans-Atlantic television transmission. It was on July 23, 1962, via "the talking satellite," TelStar. There had been long silences and moments of discomfort, Cronkite said. "But eventually the Statue of Liberty showed up on European TVs and the Eiffel Tower on screens in the United States and Canada."

The next afternoon (European time; morning in America) there were linkages via TelStar — or attempted linkages — between a number of American cities "twinned" with European ones.

Helsinki's twin for this event was to be Madison, Wisconsin. And I, boy diplomat ..."acting assistant information officer" ... working in the American Cultural Center of the U.S. Information Service in downtown Helsinki ... had been given responsibility for this some weeks earlier.

My boss' boss, USIS' director in Helsinki, was a Mr. Peterson. This was Mr. Peterson's first assignment abroad; he had for several years been a Washington-based civil servant. He was ambitious. He wanted to be noticed back in Washington. So aggressive and self-promoting was he that the Ambassador eventually sent him home. But not before he had me kill the rector of the University of Helsinki.

There had been a problem from the very beginning of this endeavor. Helsinki and Madison had been twinned for it because the rector, a renowned and revered Classicist as well as a wartime Prime Minister, had some months before visited the United States, at our Embassy's invitation. While there he had visited the University of Wisconsin. And while there, he had called upon his counterpart, the President of the University of Wisconsin.

"You go tell Rector Linkomies to do this," Mr. Peterson told me. "It'll be a huge story."

I was 26, not much older than Rector Linkomies' students. And students did NOT simply drop in on the Rektor Magnifikus. In fact, he was the last of the University's rectors to expect students to bow deeply before him whenever they met.

Mr. Peterson dismissed my reservations. "Do it!" he said.

I asked our cultural attaché, Dr. Frank Lewand, to help. Dr. Lewand was in his 50's, a pipe smoker like the rector, and he had been involved in arranging Rector Linkomies' visit to the United States.

Dr. Lewand's Finnish secretary made the appointment, and the two of us entered the rector's book-lined office. We took seats in tasteful leather-covered chairs.

There was a long silence as the two gentlemen fiddled with their respective pipes. "When are we going to tell him that this is going to be one of the biggest stories ever?" I wondered.

"Fine weather," said Dr. Lewand.

"A bit wet," said Rector Linkomies.

"Do you remember your visit to the University of Wisconsin?" asked Dr. Lewand eventually.

"Oh yes; Oh yes ...."

"And your visit with University President Winslow?"

"Oh yes. Oh yes. Of course, Dr. Lewand."

"Well, we wondered whether you might like to speak with President Winslow ... to thank him for your visit, perhaps."

"Thank him? On the telephone?"

"Yes, on the telephone."

"Oh, that won't be necessary, Dr. Lewand. I thanked him already, with a letter. And as you know, trans-Atlantic telephone calls are quite expensive.

"No; I don't think that will be necessary," the rector repeated, blowing another puff into the already smoky room.

"Well actually," said Dr. Lewand, "this telephone call wouldn't cost anything at all.

"It seems that scientists are putting a sort of 'satellite' up in orbit. And this thing can transmit telephone calls. So because it's new, and this is the first time, they've said that you and President Winslow could speak for free."

"Interesting," said the rector ... whose voice indicated that it wasn't, really.

Amidst the long pauses, Dr. Lewand led the rector to agree that, since "the telephone conversation" would be "free," there was no reason he should not accept the offer. We would let him know when and where it would be. Little did he know.

That was still the time of black and white television, and bright, hot klieg lights even for news shots.

When Rector Linkomies arrived at the appointed hour, he found that the "conversation" was not to be inside our Cultural Center offices, but in front of our building, on Helsinki's main street ...and via a phone on a stand behind which he would sit, literally surrounded by lights, cameras and shoulder-to-shoulder journalists and technicians.

It was awful:

The connections didn't work.

"Hallo, hallo?," repeated the septuagenarian classical scholar again and again, perspiring profusely.

"Hallo? Hallo?"

And when a garbled American voice finally came onto the phone, it wasn't from Madison, Wisconsin, at all. And it wasn't U-Wisconsin President Winslow. It was a call that was supposed to have gone somewhere else.

Eventually a Madison connection was established.

"Thank you having me at your university," said the rector softly. And then the call was cut off. The 20 minutes during which Telstar's orbit was over the Atlantic had elapsed.

I found a cab to take Rector Linkomies home. My boss, Mr. Peterson, pronounced it all a Great Success.

Two days later, the morning papers announced the death of Rector Linkomies.

He had collapsed with a heart attack the day before.

No obituary made a connection between the "telephone call" and the gentleman's death.

But I did.

My first K.I.A.: Killed in Action. And it wouldn't, unfortunately, be the last.

Off to Africa

The reverie of that first Foreign Service assignment in Helsinki would have to end, of course. It was for a foreordained eleven months. Sometime in the autumn of 1962 I was told that my next assignment would be to the West African nation of Sierra Leone.

I dutifully went to the British Council library and read everything that could be read in Finland about Sierra Leone: its history, its various tribes, its governance. The change I would be experiencing could hardly be more extreme. So I fortified myself with all that I knew I'd be missing: the cold, the winter, the crayfish fests, the cross country skiing, the saunas, the friendships, the sheer exuberance.

The time to pack arrived; the goodbye party was scheduled. And less than a week before my departure a colleague called from the Embassy:

"I thought you were going to Sierra Leone, Bob?" he said.

"That's right."

"So why do your orders say 'Mogadishu'?" he said.

"I have no idea," I croaked. "Where's that????"

"Never heard of it," he said. "In South America, maybe????"

A search of the office atlas revealed Mogadishu to be on the opposite side of the African continent, protruding into the Red Sea and the Indian Ocean. At the fun farewell party, at which I was made an "honorary member" of the Finnish National Union of Students, that's about all that I could tell anyone about the place to which I was headed. And that was still about all I knew about my new home when I arrived there several days later after stops in West Berlin (where the Wall had gone up just a few months before) and in Athens where I (1) presented my heavy Finnish woolen overcoat to a surprised Orthodox monk, and (2) left a shoe somewhere in the cave-like hovel in Plaka, on the side of the Acropolis, into which a raucous dishwater blonde who had picked me up in a bistro had invited me to share the remaining hours of my last night in Europe.

"President Kennedy's Been Shot"

But as it turned out, I would be back in Helsinki a few months later, in mid- November 1963. This was for several reasons: my abject, self-pitying loneliness through those first months in Somalia; my need to share my miseries with my sorely-missed Finnish friends, and ... quite awkwardly ... my intention to extract myself from my long-distance engagement to Vickan.

The first thing that happened was that, when I sorrowfully related to my friends my experiences thus far in Somalia, these tales — several of which will be shared here as well — evoked not the intended heartfelt pity, but great roaring guffaws of laughter! I thus began to learn a lesson of much help through difficult times in later years: "Comedy," as Carol Burnett said, "is tragedy plus time."

But breaking up with the sweet, lovely, beguiling and long-tressed Vickan, with whom I was staying in her parents' Helsinki apartment (after several days in a rustic cabin on an isolated lake) was, unavoidably, going to be painful ... and messy ... and probably even stupid. But suddenly a real tragedy — a national tragedy, a global tragedy — made this and any other personal troubles become minuscule in comparison.

The night before I was to fly back to Somalia, Vickan and I were at a "sauna party" with Finnish friends. The women were upstairs fixing the food; it was the guys' turn in the sauna. There was snow on the ground, so we had the whole works: the sweating, the rolling in the snow; the sweating again. Then beer, and more chatting.

But the sauna door opened. A head poked in, and one of the women said:

"President Kennedy's been shot!!!!!!"

That was before satellite television. So the rest of the evening was, in shared shock and grief, spent around a radio, with my Finnish friends translating for me each new tidbit. And then the President was dead.

That was horrible enough. But in Finland it was perhaps perceived as even worse: Vice President Lyndon Johnson had visited Helsinki just a few weeks before and, as I had been hearing since my return, had made absolutely no friends either for himself or his country. Both he and Lady Bird had behaved in ways which both my Finnish friends and my Embassy colleagues considered reprehensible. I had repeatedly been asked: "How can you have such a wonderful President, and such a horrible man as Vice President?" And now that "horrible man" was America's President ... and the "Free World's" leader.

It was late November in Finland: dark, cold, foreboding. And President Kennedy, the beloved John F. Kennedy, was dead. His beautiful wife was widowed; Carolyn and John-John fatherless. And a loud, drawling Texan with neither grace nor manners was his successor.

There was no other subject of conversation, nor of thought, for the rest of the night. And the next morning, when Vickan awoke me, the first question ... and every other exchange ... was also about the tragedy.

I took a trolley to the airport bus. In every Helsinki store window there was a portrait of Kennedy, draped in black. Where had they come from? Could any other death have been so universally mourned?

There was silence in the trolley and in the bus. When people realized that I was American, they came to express, some in tears, their loss ... and sympathy.

I was in London that night. It was the same.

The next night was in Nairobi. Also there.

In Mogadishu, lacking a written language, television, and most other links to, and understanding of, an outside world, the loss seemed less evident. But that was misleading. When we later showed the beautiful filmed tribute "JFK: Years of Lightening, Day of Drums," our Somali guests ... educated abroad in Europe or the U.S. ... were also in tears. There have since been a number of moments shared by most of mankind: the Apollo 11 landing, World Cups, the fall of Saigon, the end of the Berlin Wall, 9/11. But never since, I believe, has the world shared an emotion so completely and unreservedly as when an assassin took John Kennedy from us on November 23, 1963. Lyndon Johnson's manner appealed to few abroad; Vietnam was to turn much of world opinion against us. Nixon also appealed to but a few, and there was Watergate. Jimmy Carter earned his current reputation abroad not for his Presidency, but for his actions and commitment afterward. Reagan's appeal was far from universal. Clinton's stature abroad was probably greater than at home.

George W. Bush polarized Americans ...and almost without exception appalled and frightened even friends abroad. Not until our election of Barack Obama did an American president again have something of the aura abroad of the brief Kennedy Presidency. But until then, it had been a long downhill slog.

Somalia, 1963-65

Welcome to a Very, Very Different Place

Of the many places in which I lived and worked, none seems more remarkable today than Somalia. Most of the other experiences could be re-created in some way: should I return there, much would appear unchanged. In some former hometowns, I might possibly find a geezer or geezerette whom I knew there, years ago. And in each of the capitals, I could (at least theoretically) stop by the Embassy, find an individual doing work today similar to that which I did there then, and compare notes.

Not so in Somalia. There has been no Embassy of any country in Mogadishu since 1992. There has been no government there for at least as long. Different warlords, different clans, control different parts of the place. Much has apparently returned to the nomadic existences of pre-colonial times., albeit with 21st century violence. At least three regions claim sovereignty in their areas: Puntland on the Horn itself; Somaliland along the northern coast, and whichever chieftains in Mogadishu and elsewhere claim to rule in the south.

One can only speculate, in fact, on how things may now be in that melancholy place. Journalists rarely go there: several reporters have been killed. There are few if any aid workers or foreigners of any sort. Cell phones, I understand, may be the single technological "advance"; cell phones and weapons. But most or all of the "advances" ... the "improvements" ... the "developments" which we were contributing/donating/enabling/financing back in the early '60s have vanished.

In retrospect, that period — about 1961 to 1968 or so — may have been, at least in Western/developed terms, the high point of Somali history. But what we were doing there — the Peace Corps, the teacher training schools, the agricultural projects, the wells, the police and military training — probably only touched the surface, the veneer; hardly affecting either Somali culture or the lives of most of its citizens.

When I arrived in Mogadishu in early 1963, the country had been united and independent for less than three years. Well: even "united" was disputable. Somali nomads wandered through much of the Horn of Africa, and not just in the areas which had become the Somali Republic. The country would have been at least twice as big had it included the largely Somali-populated neighboring areas of Kenya, Ethiopia and French Somaliland. But uniting and governing what had been the Italian colony (and then, after World War II, a United Nations trusteeship) of Somalia, and the former British protectorate of Somaliland, was challenging enough.

For a start, because there was no agreed upon written form for the Somali language, all written communication had to be in one of the two colonial languages, Italian or English, or in the language of the Koran: Arabic. There had been, at Independence, only two small secondary schools in the country: one in Mogadishu teaching in Italian to an Italian curriculum, the other in the north, in Sheik, teaching in English, to the British General Certificate of Education. The Egyptians had then started a high school in Mogadishu. It taught in Arabic, to an Egyptian curriculum.

Only some four or five percent of the Somali population was thought to be literate, and few of these commanded more than one of these three foreign languages. Thus, in the Education Ministry, with which I dealt, the Minister was a graduate of an Italian university, and thus wrote his notes and correspondence in Italian. His number two, the Director General, was British educated. His notes and correspondence were in English. An American Peace Corps Volunteer translated for them, and thus also for the Education Ministry staffers who, like their bosses, were literate in only the one or the other.

It's hard to know where to start to describe the strangeness of the place. Never have I been in a place in which the cultural gap was so unbreachable: I didn't know of a single foreigner, whether American,

European, Asian or African, who felt they had made during their tour, and would miss when they left, a single Somali friend (as opposed to "contact").

Except with the very few Somalis who had experienced life elsewhere, finding common ground — whether experiences, interests, enthusiasms or concerns — was almost excruciating. It was hardly an exaggeration to claim, as I sometimes did, that there were actually only two conversational topics that worked: (1) the weather, which hardly changed anyway, and (2) the Somali language, which we didn't understand and which they couldn't really explain. Almost anywhere else, one would reasonably quickly, in a conversation, find some topic: a musical group, a historical figure, a sport, a movie, a personality, on which one could then share, and compare, views. But not here.

I was the loneliest that I had ever been (although later, in Vietnam, I would long for several of the friendships with non-Somalis which I eventually made). The ogres of USIA's personnel department had ripped me from the wonderfully hedonistic paradise of Helsinki to send me to this awful spot. I had arrived in my Finnish woolen suit and a synthetic, sauna-like shirt. I had no Somali visa, it having not occurred to anyone in Helsinki that such a thing was even obtainable. George Miller, my new boss, met me at Mogadishu's torrid, shabby, dusty, airport (the plane from Rome came only once each week). "No visa, can't enter," said the immigration man. Nothing that George could say could change his mind. "Too many people coming with no visas. No respect for our country. Can't come in."

George ruled out my getting back on the Alitalia flight doubting, probably, that I'd ever willingly return. Instead, I was to go to jail. This would presumably be temporary, however: only the national chief of police could liberate me and he, it was said, would not be returning to town until late evening. George agreed to this, and went off to find someone in the Embassy who could speak with the police chief upon his return. Meanwhile, sweating pounds per minute in my long pants and plastic shirt, I waited miserably on a bench in a corner at the airport. No one arrived to take me to jail, and eventually George returned with permission to take me to town. An inauspicious beginning to what was clearly going to be a very, very, long two years.

Young Bob Dickerman (well, I was 27) was to be the "public affairs assistant" of USIS Mogadishu. We were three American USIS officers, working with perhaps a dozen Somali colleagues in a downtown building catercorner from the Embassy itself. The library, for which I was responsible, was on the ground floor. Our offices were on the second floor. Behind the building, walled-in, was an open area where we showed films once per week. And behind that was the "film section," where two Somali staffers cared for our projectors and our collection of 16mm films.

In addition to the library, I was responsible for the film program, our exhibits, our occasional visiting performing groups or lecturers, and our scholarship program.

I inherited the house of my predecessor, so moved in that first day without a transition through a hotel room. It was a compact, four-room masonry house on the hillside overlooking the city and the Indian Ocean. It faced a dusty camel trail leading out of town. The barren yard was sand; there was a scrub tree or two. The house came with my "boy," Aden, and a round-the-clock guard service. The latter, tribal fellows with spears whom the Administrative Officer had been told might likely be breaking into our houses unless paid to guard them, were usually asleep. The danger, as I experienced more than once, was in awakening them. They would then come charging at me with those spears, apparently realizing, at the very last minute, that this pale-skinned individual was likely the resident they were supposed to be protecting.

I found having my first servant, Aden, awkward. He was in my house, so was he my friend, my guest, my companion? Or what? I solved the dilemma by having him there as little as possible. He did the shopping, served my breakfast and lunch, did the cleaning and laundry, and then was free. Understandably, two years later my successor fired him immediately, judging him spoiled and lazy.

The first months were dreadfully lonely. After wonderful friendships in Helsinki, both male and female, in Mogadishu everyone that I knew was somehow related to my work, my position, and therefore a cause for caution and reserve. It was the smallest of communities. We worked together, then met again at the Embassy beach house. And next to that were the beach houses of the Italians, the Germans, and the United Nations staff. There was no one to laugh with, no one to complain to, no one to confide in ...and certainly no one to give me the sympathy that I thought I so richly deserved for having been yanked to this tropical horror from my Nordic Valhalla. A snapshot from that period shows me haggard, skinny and pale, forcing a smile while surrounded by Somali children.

My social (i.e. erotic) life had never been better than during those few short months in Helsinki. And now I found myself in a spot where female companionship, other than the local dance hall whores, seemed impossible. I knew of only three high-school-educated single women my age. One was the daughter of an Indian UN official who didn't permit her to go out un-escorted. One was our Italian secretary at USIS, who already had an Embassy fiancé. And the third, the target of every other expatriate bachelor's attention, was an Elizabeth Taylor look-alike, the daughter of an Italian businessman.

When it finally became my turn to take this dark-eyed beauty with her hourglass figure to dinner at the Croce del Sud, I laid on the compliments. "You Italian women are so beautiful!" I gushed. And then the mouth kept driveling: "But why do so many later become so fat???"

The shapely signorina glared. She laid down her knife and fork. She stood up. She marched out without another word, leaving me wanting to kill myself.

Not until sometime later did I see her mother: una donna molto grande.

Molto, molto, grande in fact. But that was absolutely no consolation.

Embassy Row

Downtown Mogadishu was dusty, hot and crumbling. No building was higher than two stories, and all were made of a poor quality of cement. Bleaching, peeling yellow was the basic color. And fading whitewash. The streets were paved in the center of town: this was the national capital, after all, and there were sidewalks. Shops opened out onto the sidewalks. Few had doors, but the entrances could be closed with metal shutters. Ceiling fans droned in most.

The American Embassy was one block north of the center of town. The building had until recently ... until Independence three years before ... been the city's preeminent brothel. Just behind it were the warrens of Shengani, home to dozens of lessor brothels and scores of prostitutes.

The Embassy's entranceway was open to the sidewalk. To the right was a staircase which went upstairs, to the left a staircase heading down. At the nexus was Abdullah, facing the sidewalk and peering over the Embassy's antique telephone switchboard. He answered the infrequent incoming calls and directed Embassy visitors either upstairs or down.

Abdullah had also been the maitre d' when the Embassy was still a brothel (we were leasing it from the Madam). Some who came to the entranceway had non-diplomatic interests. These Abdullah simply directed around the building, to the Shengani offerings.

Proposing

There were no telephone connections between Somalia and the outside world. So when I decided to propose to a (the?) Helsinki girlfriend, it was going to have to be done via a shortwave radio connection.

Vickan and I had been exchanging letters ... but these took at least two, and sometimes three, weeks to make the trip between just north of the Equator, to just south of the Arctic Circle, or reverse. Serendipitously, however, we were in the same time zone.

Our communication was always out-of-kilter; each of us responding to the other's questions, signs, mutterings, concerns, worries or imaginings, long after the other had, days or weeks ago, either answered or changed direction. There was flirting from each end. I don't know how she felt, but the lonelier I became there in Mogadishu, the more precious and beautiful and erotic became the memories of the (very few, actually) dates which we'd had in beautiful Finland.

So I telegraphed her that I wanted to call her on such and such a day, noting that it would have to be between 8 and 10 am since it was only during those hours that the Mogadishu radio transmitter maintained a link to Rome ... from whence our voices would travel not by shortwave radio, but by wire.

Lovely Vickan telegraphed back that it would have to be before 9:15 am, as she would have to depart for an exam. I took my motor-scooter to the hilltop on the edge of town ... a sanddune, actually

...where the antenna, transmitter, and the concrete block office of Somalia's wireless service was located. I told them, as required, that I wanted to book a call to Helsinki at 8 am on that date. "No problem," he said (all of this being conducted in his broken, and my much worse, Italian).

But there were.

I arrived at 8 and was shown to a seat at a small table with a microphone, facing the ear-phoned technician with his various dials, wires and apparati. I was also given earphones. It was already getting very hot. But a fan buzzed.

"No connection," he said, fiddling the buttons and calling "Roma? Roma? Roma?"

"No connection still," he said, a good 15 minutes later.

And again, a half an hour after that. Vickan would be leaving soon. And, having steeled myself through the long night to make this scary proposal, I wondered whether I'd ever be able — or even desire — to do it on another day, should this attempt fail.

Finally "hallo Roma," and we were halfway there. But there seemed to be problems making the landline connection between Rome and Helsinki. It was 9:10. Then the technician told me that we were "on."

"Hello Vickan!!!!!!"

"Louder," said the technician.

"HELLO VICKAN!!!!!!!!!!!!!!!!"

"LOUDER!," said the technician.

"HELLO VICKAN!!!!!!!!!!!!!!!!!!!!!!!!!!," I yelled.

"Hello Bob!," said the earphones, faintly.

"HOW ARE YOU, VICKAN?," I yelled ...loudly enough, I thought, to be heard down in the town.

"I'm fine, how are you Bob??????????"

There was some breakup; I guess we were both trying to speak at the same time, and a voice from Rome (how many people are listening to this?????????, I thought) said, in English, that we had to say "OVER" each time that we had finished speaking. Only a couple of minutes to go ....

"Bob, I have to catch my bus for my exam."

Then, only the crackling of the shortwave.

"Say 'OVER'" said the voice in Rome.

"I have to catch the bus for my exam Over" said she. "OVER!!!!!!" said I.

"NO," said Rome. "Now you talk, Mogadishu."

"VICKAN," I yelled, as embarrassed as I have ever been in my life; the tech's bland face just across the equipment from mine,

"VICKAN, WILL YOU MARRY ME?????????????????"

"OH, UHHH ....OVER."

"Do what ....Over?

"I SAID: VICKAN, WILL YOU MARRY ME?????????????????

"OVER."

"Oh ...okay. All right. When??? How??? No, No, I have to go now. Is that all? Oh ....over"

"Yes, well, that's all. Okay Vickan, Bye Bye ....uh, over."

And she was gone. And lovely Rome and Europe with her.

Was I sweating so profusely because of the heat? The ordeal? The pain? The pleasure?

"Va bene," said the tech. "Okay." And took back his earphones.

His equipment continued its squealing and static.

I stepped out into the scorching sunlight. "What in the world," I shuddered, "have I done now??????????"

The President's Pants

It's a bit hard to be a foreign propagandist when the country you're in has no written language, and neither you nor your fellow Embassy officers speak the local language. Some of the Peace Corps kids learned some conversational Somali eventually, and there was a linguistic anthropologist with the USAID mission who had a fair command of the tongue. But there was also the enormous cultural divide: there was so very little that we foreigners — whether North American, European, Asian, Middle Eastern or other African — had in common with Somalis.

So, whether propagandists or simply interested visitors, communication was a challenge.

At the United States Information Service, of course, we were propagandists ...although we would never have used the word. "Information." "Culture." "Educational Exchange." "The Library." "English Teaching." All honorable and needed. One could do these things with some pride, and I did.

But nevertheless, there were certain points that we ...that I ... was supposed to get over. One was that AMERICA IS HELPING SOMALIA. And we were: with a considerable USAID program, drilling wells, building schools, training teachers, developing infrastructure, sending students to the U.S. .

But basically, how to communicate?

Photographs were one way, and I was responsible for the glass display cases on the front of the Embassy. Here we displayed 8x10 black & white photos of AMERICANS HELPING SOMALIA: digging, planting, giving, teaching. Although as Muslims Somalis were generally opposed to images, and although a foreigner could get into great trouble, and even killed, by photographing Somalis who did not want their "image captured," the photographs in our display cases were quite popular. Most by-passers stopped to study them. And when Abdi Issa, "my" photographer, changed the photos, groups collected to see what was new.

But one Sunday when I was home, Abdi phoned me excitedly:

"Mr. Dickerman! Many people at our photo boards!!!! Very angry! Shouting and saying the boards must be smashed!"

"Why, Abdi, why???"

"Because, they say it is 'insult to Somalia.'"

"What is an insult, Abdi?"

"You know, Mr. Dickerman, there is a photograph of the President at a dedication?!"

"Yes, Abdi; a nice picture. What about it?"

"They say it is an insult to Somalia. They very angry. Very dangerous, Mr. Dickerman!"

"But why is it an insult, Abdi?"

"Because people say picture shows the President with his pants (fly) open!"

"But it doesn't, does it?"

"I don't think so, Mr. Dickerman. But everyone knows that the President's pants often open.

"So maybe so."

"So what to do now, Abdi?"

"Take out the pictures right away. They going to burn the Embassy! Many people! Very angry!"

And so the brave Abdi — one of the broad nosed, large-lipped

"Somali Bantus" whom the Somalis regarded as "slaves" — did exactly that.

And we decided to let the exhibit boxes be photoless for the coming weeks.

The Claremont

The early 60's were a time of great optimism through much of Africa. Three dozen or so countries became independent, freed of the "yoke" (as it was then described) of British, French or Belgian colonialism. Prominent among those who assumed power in these new nations were the handfuls of individuals who had been educated abroad.

The first Ambassadors of some of these countries were particularly impressive: articulate, intelligent, cosmopolitan graduates of the Sorbonne, Oxford, Cambridge, Harvard and so forth. The Kennedy administration found them congenial soulmates: President Kennedy himself apparently enjoyed hours with them.

As "cultural presentations" at that time, the State Department was generally sending to Africa performers who could travel light: harmonica players, small dance groups, some jazz. The African Ambassadors in Washington apparently considered these choices "degrading." We should be sending to Africa, they argued, the same cultural showpieces that we would send to Europe.

Thus it was that the Claremont String Quartet ...then said to be second in renown only to the Julliard ...arrived on the weekly Alitalia flight at Mogadishu International Airport. Four fellows, three of them Jewish in this very fundamentalist Islamic society, one of them a former New York State junior tennis champ, and all enthused about this first stop on their scheduled multi-country African tour.

I was their "control officer", responsible for their care, planning, preparations, publicity, transportation, hospitality and general mothering.

I had sensed that there might be some cultural disconnect when affixing posters about their two concerts to poles and scrubby trees throughout the town. The posters bore a photograph of the quartet with their instruments, and announced, in Italian (the colonial language of the southern part of the country) the time of the two concerts in the "university auditorium."

Only a fraction of the populace could read. But there was considerable interest in the posters. They crowded around at each stop.

"Who's the poet?", they asked my USIS colleague, Ismail.

"Poet? No poet. These are musicians."

"No poet? Only accompaniment???!" And they moved away, disappointedly.

And then came the concert. In spite of heat in the high 90's, the basketball court-sized hall, filled with folding chairs, was packed ... with virtually every white face in that city: every Warsaw Pact diplomat, every Italian colonial, every European official, every Peace Corps volunteer.

There were three black faces. That in the front row belonged to the nation's single PhD, the president of the (not-yet-commenced) "university." He was the host, and said "kind words."

The other two, in the back row, were "ladies of the evening" who had misunderstood.

They left soon. The Claremont, dripping with sweat, performed magnificently. The audience ... especially, it seemed, the Communist diplomats ... applauded enthusiastically and gratefully. The university president shook hands with our Ambassador, and left as well. The next night, there was not a single black face.

And too bad, too. The Quartet, thinking that the problem was perhaps that some of the music was too slow, played only first and final movements on that second notable evening. The sweaty packed house loved it. Another victory in the cultural wars.

The Lost Field Marshall

The night before the return of the weekly Alitalia flight that would take the Claremont String Quartet to Nairobi, its Field Marshall went missing.

Some might have thought this gent the second violinist. But he was determined, at least with me, that he not be perceived as second to anyone, but fully as worthy as any of his three colleagues. I could refer to him, he said, as "The Field Marshall." And I did.

The quartet was staying at one of the town's two hotels. This was on the opposite side of Shengani, the brothel district, from the Embassy. I had taken them through it on an occasion or two.

But when I arrived at the hotel at breakfast time to fetch the group for their trip to the airport, the Field Marshall was missing. He had gone out for a stroll the evening before. And apparently hadn't returned. On the scale of things, this was No Small Crisis.

The most likely ... or at least more searchable ...spot seemed to be Shengani. I enlisted Abdullah, the Embassy receptionist and former brothel maitre d', and we went forth, through the narrow little alleyways, asking about the Field Marshall.

A man of his description had in fact been seen the night before, and we eventually climbed a narrow, filthy staircase to a doorframe closed with a musty curtain. Behind it, seated and chatting with the resident, was our Marshall.

They had been speaking all night, he explained. The lady, he said, had once had a German boyfriend ...and had thus developed quite erroneous (i.e., positive) perceptions of Germans. He had spent the night, the Field Marshall said, correcting these misperceptions. After all, hadn't Uncle Sam sent him to Africa to counter misperceptions?????

Arni

In the early 1960's, Gamal Abdul Nasser's Egypt broadcast virulently anti-Israeli programming throughout much of the Middle East and Africa. Radio Cairo's Somali Service combined political rants with popular Egyptian and other Arabic music. In a land without a written language or publications, shortwave radio, received on the new transistor radios, was a powerful and influential medium.

President Kennedy's and Sergeant Shriver's calls for idealistic young Americans to join the Peace Corps enthused recent college graduates throughout the country, but none moreso than Californians and Jews. The first Peace Corps contingent to arrive in Somali, "Somalia One," was, like its counterparts in other countries, thus disproportionately Californian and Jewish.

Arni Greenblatt was a Volunteer who was both. Assigned to teach English for two years in a desolate village in the northern Somali bush, Arni was sitting around a campfire one evening with several of his students. They were consummate listeners to Radio Cairo.

"Mr. Greenblatt," said one. "We hear terrible things on the radio about Jews. We are very worried about them. Some might come here to attack us. But none of us has ever seen a Jew. We don't know what they look like.

"Mr. Greenblatt, you have been to many places and seen many things. Tell us: what do Jews look like?"

"Well," said Arni. "First of all, they're green."

"Ah," said the students. "Then it will be easy."

(Oddly, the Somalis seemed not to make the connection between the Jews of whom they were warned on Radio Cairo, and the occasional "Hebrew" merchants who dealt in gold and other items in Mogadishu and some of the coastal towns. The Hebrews were simply part of the melange of Bahrainis, Yemeni, Goans, Lebanese and Greeks whose various diasporas, and dhows, had deposited them through the centuries along the Indian Ocean coast.)

Teaching

Teaching in the rudimentary Somali schools, as most of the Peace Corps Volunteers did, was challenging. And not just because of the physical conditions. Much more challenging than the lack of virtually everything that an American takes for granted was the isolation, the lack of interlocutors (on most subjects), the lack of privacy ...the sheer conspicuousness of being the single outsider in a small, interrelated community of people with whom one shared very little.

And then there was the issue of Credibility as a teacher. If one wasn't careful, one could say things ...in class or out ... which would put one's very sanity to question.

The shape of our world was such an issue. Everyone knew it was flat; everyone could see that; all evidence proved it. So what kind of nut would think it round? And how could such a nut have been sent to teach in our school????

Most of the Volunteers viewed this pragmatically: why put one's credentials as a teacher of other, perhaps more important subjects, to question just because of this pretty irrelevant cosmological one?

But one of the Volunteers in the North ... I forget his name ... teaching in the highlands across from the Gulf of Aden, took a different approach. One night he thought he would prove the roundness of our world. Joining the group around the fire that night was Ibrahim. Ibrahim, like a goodly number of Somali men, had gotten himself to Aden, from which he had then sailed as a merchant seaman.

"Ibrahim," said the Volunteer, "you took a ship that headed northwest, through the Suez Canal?"

"Yes," said Ibrahim.

"And then you sailed to the west, through Gibraltar, and then north to England?"

"Yes," Ibrahim said.

"And then you took another ship, and sailed west to America, and then west again through the Panama Canal to the Pacific Ocean?"

"Yes, I did," said Ibrahim.

"And then you sailed west again, to Japan and Singapore, and then west again until you came back to Aden"

"Yes," said Ibrahim.

"Well see!" said the Volunteer triumphantly, "you kept sailing westward and westward until you had sailed all the way around the world! You proved, Ibrahim, that the world is round!"

But Ibrahim was astonished that the American teacher could make such a statement.

"Yes," he said, looking around the group. "I have traveled very much. I have seen much of the world. And everywhere, brothers and sisters, it is flat."

Flying the Crocodile Home

I no longer remember what the reason was. But whatever it was, three of us found ourselves flying in a small plane one day from Mogadishu to a small town on the Ethiopian border. I think it was Dhuusamareeb ... which the linguistic anthropologist at the USAID mission said translated into "Smells like a fart from which one cannot escape."

In any case, we flew over miles of bush, following tracks through it: a road, actually, but without traffic. We saw camels and giraffes. And could appreciate, better than one could on the ground, how scarce the watering holes were, and how far it was between them. Without these, neither the camels nor the nomads could live for long.

When we approached the village, the pilot flew over it, dipping his wing, to alert the District Chief to meet us on the cleared strip of bush that served as an airstrip. As he dipped his wing, tracers of bullets passed by us. "Damn" said the pilot.

He dipped toward the landing strip, and now we could see the machine gun firing at us. It continued to do so as we taxied down the strip.

A Land Rover arrived in a cloud of dust and pulled alongside us. It was the District Chief.

"You are very lucky," he said. "I have saved your lives>"

"Saved our lives?" said the pilot. "Your men could have killed us."

"But I stopped them," said the District Chief. "I stopped them before you came to a stop. They would surely have hit you then. But I stopped them."

The previous week, he said later, the same soldiers had tried to shoot down a passing Alitalia passenger plane. Same reason, he said:

"They thought it was an Ethiopian fighter plane attacking."

We may have been going there to pick up an ill Peace Corps volunteer. I don't recall. But while there, in the District Chief's care, his view of the shooting seemed to change. Perhaps he thought his superiors in Mogadishu would not be impressed by our tale.

In any case, he became almost apologetic. We were given gifts, including a very dry and very lengthy and old crocodile skin. This we lashed to the bottom of the plane, and returned to the capital without further adventures.

Traffic Lights

There had been no traffic lights in Mogadishu when I had arrived. Instead, at three or four intersections, there were Somali caliberri, elegantly white-uniformed policemen with sun helmets, white gloves, whistles and batons. They moved beautifully. It must have been one of the more sought-after jobs in the police department. The young ladies, in any case, seemed to love the show.

But eventually the Italians gave a traffic light, which replaced the caliberro in the city's center, a block from my office above the American Library. This, as I recall, was a single device hanging in the middle of the intersection. It had the red light on the top, then yellow, then green. It hung in the middle of the intersection, with its lights facing in four directions.

All well and good, except that the Russians soon gave a traffic light as well ... or more correctly, a set of four lights.

These went up a block or so to the west. But on this corner there were now four lights, one on each corner, instead of the one hanging above the intersection's center. The driver was to follow the instruction, as I recall, of the light on the opposite corner. On these Russian lights, though, the colors were reversed: green on top, then yellow, and red on the bottom. There was no little confusion. And the groups of amused onlookers at each intersection grew. It seemed to be great fun to watch the colors change, the cars stop or not stop, the drivers self-conscious.

And eventually a third light was given, by yet another country. And it, as I recall, employed yet another system. There was no end to progress.

The Post Office

Somalia's post office also needed to be brought to a standard befitting a now-independent country. But three years after Independence, there still were, in effect, two different postal systems. Although they used a shared currency, the post offices in the northern part of the country, former British Somaliland, used ounces; those in the southern, formerly Italian portion, used grams.

In any case, a pair of postal experts arrived, dispatched by the International Postal Union in Geneva. They were a rather comically-appearing pair, like Mutt & Jeff: one tall and slim, the other short, hirsute and brawny, both from the Balkans. I chatted with them at the beach one day:

"It's amazing," the tall one said. "When they prepare the outgoing mail at the Mogadishu post office, they sort it into a wooden cabinet with many small ....what do you call them? ... chubby holes. These chubby holes are identified; there's one for every major destination in Italy. At the lower right hand corner is one which says 'Il Resto del Mondo' — the rest of the world."

The Spider Men

There are people on city streets in most lands which, while initially shocking, one eventually becomes inured to. In Mogadishu it was the "spidermen." I no longer recall the name of their disease. But they had lost, because of it, command of their legs. These they dragged behind them, lying prone, extending their hands before them, then pulling their bodies forward. The lucky ones had shower clogs to increase the friction; others did not. There were always a number on Mogadishu's central sidewalks, begging. They begged most plaintively when a white person approached. And especially so if one had given something when one last passed by. The answer, for most of us, was thus to walk past, seeming not to see them.

There were only three "newspapers" in the country: all weeklies, and all published by the Ministry of Information. One was in Arabic, one in Italian and one in English (there being then no agreed-upon written form for the Somali language).

"Spidermen a Disgrace to the Country" proclaimed a page one article in The Somali News one week. In newly-independent Somalia, the paper said, such aberrations in the very heart of the national capital ...begging, slithering along on the proud nation's sidewalks ...were unacceptable. It had to stop.

And indeed, it did, for a while. Trucks belonging to the police ...or maybe it was the army ... picked up the spidermen, loaded them in the back ...and drove them westward to the Ethiopian border. It was weeks before the spidermen, perhaps having dragged themselves all the way, began reappearing on the city's streets.

But by then the newspapers had discovered a new "disgrace." "The students," it seemed, were lolling about in the city's center, bothering folks, and generally giving the proud new nation a bad name.

The trucks had again appeared, loaded as many students as they could find, and taken them westward to the Ethiopian border. The students returned more quickly.

My (Only) Diplomatic Coup

I was an American diplomat for 30 years. But only once did I achieve a diplomatic coup. I was only 28, and it was in my second Foreign Service tour. After that, it was all down hill.

Not that there was any recognition of what I had done. But this will take some explaining:

The Somali flag was a five-pointed white star on a field of United Nations blue. The blue was because the southern part of the country, the former Italian colony, had been a United Nations trust territory after World War II. And the five pointed star represented the union, or more correctly the desired re-union, of the Somali people. These — in fact, not just national myth — had been divided into five parts by a long ago treaty of the colonial powers. Only two of these parts — the former Italian colony, Somalia, and the former British protectorate, British Somaliland — had been united at independence. Still "subjugated," in the Somali view, were their kinsmen in the Northern Frontier District of Kenya, French Somaliland (Djibouti), and the huge Ogaden region of Ethiopia. Every future Somali government would have this revanchist aim, although this first may have held to it most unreservedly. Not a week went by without the radio station, and the three Government-published papers, blasting the British, French and Ethiopians for their continuing subjugation of the (overwhelming) Somali majorities in the three still-unfree territories.

Thus the five pointed star on the national flag: the five divided parts united in independent Somalia.

And thus the setting for my Diplomatic Coup. It happened this way:

The Somali government had taken to agitating for the island of Socrata, some miles south of the Arabian peninsula and a good many more miles east of the Somali coast. Socrata was, the government, its radio, and its papers said, rightfully and historically Somalia's. Its incorporation by the British into its Aden Protectorate was wrong and illegal. And that wrong was to be righted.

It took me years to begin to enjoy cocktail parties, and those in Somalia I disliked especially. Fortunately, they were rare (the Somali men were as ill-at-ease as I, and their wives, if they came, were utterly out of place).

But this one was at my boss', and the Somali guests were "our" Somalis in the media and information and education ministries. I found myself in awkward conversation with the Information Minister. Fumbling for a subject, and way, way out-of-line on official policy, I sputtered:

"I think it will be really interesting if you really get Socrata."

"Interesting? Why?" said the Minister.

"Because of the flag."

"What about the flag?"

"Because your flag will then have a six-pointed star."

"So?," said the Minister.

"You know, Sir: the six-pointed star, the 'Star of David'; the star on the flag of Israel."

The minister's eyes registered a bit of surprise, and someone arrived to rescue him from conversation with a mere junior officer.

But there was never, ever, another word said about Somalia's right to Socrata. Ever again. Not in the media, and not in diplomacy.

Young Dickerman had actually done something. But it wasn't something that you go around talking about.

The Two Great Powers

Few Americans have any idea how our country is perceived abroad. And I was sometimes surprised myself.

When substitute teaching an English course for Somali officials, I hung a world map on the wall and pointed to the northern part of the Western Hemisphere.

"What's this?" I asked.

"The United States of America," they chorused.

"And what's this?," I asked, pointing to South America.

"Cuba!," they chimed.

By having been so noisy and so concerned about Cuba ...and claiming that we were so threatened by it ... we had given the impression that it must be at least as large and formidable as the U.S.

I didn't have the heart to point to the tiny speck that was Cuba. The mis-impression was entirely our doing.

Presenting the Wild Boar

Wild boar was fairly common in the Somali bush, but since as Muslims the Somalis eschewed pork, they were rarely hunted.

Ambassador Torbert's wife, Anne, had apparently long wanted to serve, in proper style, a roasted boar. She had her chance when a Congressional delegation would be visiting. There would be only fellow Americans at the dinner, so it seemed a perfect opportunity.

A fine boar was shot and delivered to the Residence. A proper pit and spit was created in the back yard. The roasting started in the morning and continued through the day.

Mrs. Torbert was especially concerned that this special feast be properly presented and served. The Torberts had a very competent "boy," Mohammed, but he had never before served boar.

"Mohammed," Mrs. Torbert later recalled saying:

"Now when I ring my bell, you will roll the boar in on this cart. Understand?"

"Yes, Memsaab."

"You and the cook will have placed the boar on his back with his legs in the air. Understand, Mohammed?"

"I understand, Memsaab."

"Now: before you roll him into the dining room, you must place this apple in the boar's mouth. And use this red ribbon to tie little bows around the boar's ankles. You understand, Mohammed?"

"I understand, Memsaab," said Mohammed.

"Any questions, Mohammed?" she asked.

"No questions, Memsaab; I understand," he said.

And so it was that evening, at the Ambassador's dinner for the visiting Congressmen that, when Mrs. Torbert rang her bell, Mohammed wheeled in the cart. On it, on its back, was the well-roasted boar, his legs in the air.

And alongside the cart was Mohammed, beaming, with the apple in his mouth, and bows of red ribbon tied neatly around his wrists.

TelStar Reaches Somalia

Two years after we had in Helsinki, with so much hoopla, celebrated the trans-Atlantic communication made possible by the orbiting TelStar satellite, a worn exhibit on TelStar reached Mogadishu. With it, we were to proclaim and demonstrate our prowess, proficiency and brilliance.

The exhibit consisted of four panels with illustrations and explanations. The centerpiece was a replica (of the outside only) of TelStar. It included a little sound system. TelStar, the talking satellite, actually talked! A tape recorder was to be placed behind one of the panels, and there were two small speakers in the TelStar replica itself.

The exhibit arrived with its pre-recorded message in English. Speaking in the first person, it explained how "I" worked, and what "I" did.

But an English tape wasn't going to do me much good in Mogadishu. Very few spoke it. Italian would have been a bit more useful, but Telstar needed, I thought, to speak Somali.

I took the script to an English speaking staffer at Radio Mogadishu. I have no idea what the version which he eventually recorded said, but he did admit to considerable challenge in forcing a language of nomadic camel herders to explain travel in outer space.

Anyway, I put his tape into the machine and set up the exhibit. But first, as one always did in Africa ...whether with an idea or a project ...I "field tested" it on my "boy," Aden. I put him on the back of my motor scooter after lunch and took him to the entranceway of our library, where the exhibit would be.

I wanted him to be awed. After all: that was the whole point.

He looked at the sphere, which was perhaps a bit over two feet in diameter. He briefly scanned the photos on the exhibit panels. The tape played. Aden seemed quite unawed.

"This is a space satellite, Aden," I said.

" ... space satellite ..." he repeated.

"The Americans made this!" I said, helpfully.

" ... made this ...."

"It goes out into space and around and around the world!"

" ... around the world ...."

If Aden's reaction to our TelStar exhibit was going to be that of Somalis generally, it certainly was not going to Enhance Our Reputation.

"Aden!," I said, practically taking him by the shoulders and shaking him,

"Aden! This is like an airplane! It goes up in the sky and around and around!"

"OHHHHH!" said Aden. "OHHHH! Americans very smart ...."

"Yes, Aden, yes" I said, adding, to myself, "THAT is the point!"

"I never see such a little airplane," he said.

Duncan, Ike, and Carl Sandberg

My autumn, 1961, entering class of new Foreign Service Officers with the U. S. Information Agency was the first to be selected through the State Department's system of written and oral examinations. This was presumably a good step in terms of making us (almost, but never quite) the equals of our State FSO colleagues, but it was also at a cost.

It certainly reduced the "character quotient" of USIA's officer corps. Through the 1950's the Agency had taken on a remarkable number of accomplished, idiosyncratic, wonderful oddballs. There were old school newspapermen, folks from the theater, and a number of former Austrians, Hungarians, Poles and such. Most were folks who never would have come through the standardized, one-size-fits-all, Foreign Service Exam.

At USIS Mogadishu, we had two such. One was our information officer, Irv Pomeroy. One of his books, The Great Mouse Hunt, was a hilarious account of an over-the-Sahara expedition which he and his wife had made with Randolph Churchill and a group of Royal Marines to find the still-undemarcated southern border of Libya. It was Irv who, on a Somali weekend, borrowed the Embassy Land Rover for a picnic on a beach to the south. Unfortunately he parked too close to the water ...and returned from a hike to find the vehicle completely under a high tide. (It helped when he returned that Information Officers are, in effect, professional liars.)

But the most wonderful of all of these characters was Duncan MacDougal McDonald Emrich. Duncan was with us in Mogadishu only for a three month temporary tour. White-haired and ruddy faced, claiming to start off every morning with a fifth of bourbon, he was listed in the American Directory of Scholars under three quite different disciplines. He had been General Eisenhower's staff historian in London, and claimed to have been the single civilian who was privy to all of Ike's planning for the D-Day invasion of Normandy. He had apparently ghosted much or all of Eisenhower's Crusade in Europe. After the war he had succeeded Alan Lomax as head of the Library of Congress' renowned American Folklife Center. I've just looked up his books:

The Book of Wishes and Wishmaking; The Cowboy's Own Brand Book; The Folklore of Love and Courtship: The Charms and Divinations, Superstitions and Beliefs, Signs and Prospects of Love, Sweet Love; The Folklore of Weddings and Marriage; The Traditional Beliefs, Customs, Superstitions, Charms, and Omens of Marriage and Marriage Ceremonies ; Folklore on the American Land; In the Delta Saloon: Conversations with Residents of Virginia City, Nevada, Recorded in 1949 and 1950 ; The Lucius Beebe Reader; and The Whim-Wham Book.

Duncan was a collector ... of almost anything. He had arrived with a small suitcase, and departed with a huge collection of seashells. He'd hired boys to collect and clean them, and they were beautiful. When he departed the customs officer lifted the very heavy cases, opened them, and expressed concern:

"Is against Somali law to take away so many shells," he said.

"How much?" said Duncan. And they settled.

And his stories! When I stopped by the Eisenhower Presidential Library in Abilene, Kansas, in October 2010, I taped the following for their oral history collection:

According to Duncan, he had read one Sunday in Parade magazine, while director of the American Folklife Center, an interview with his friend and former boss, General Eisenhower. Eisenhower was then chairman of the Joint Chiefs of Staff. He had been asked by Parade to name the American whom he had not met whom he would most like to meet. Ike's response: "Carl Sandberg."

As it happened, Duncan was going to be hosting Sandberg for a reading at the Library of Congress a week or so hence. He called General Eisenhower and asked whether he'd like him to bring Sandberg to his office. "Absolutely," said the General.

So, according to Duncan, at the appointed time the two gentlemen, both white haired and ruddy faced, one in a casual shirt with a guitar over his back, went to the Pentagon making the quite unlikely claim that Five Star General Eisenhower was expecting them.

The guards didn't buy it. But they were persuaded to call ahead ... and it was indeed okay.

Duncan claimed that the closer the pair got to the Pentagon's inner sanctum, the more astonished each new perimeter's guards were that these two characters had gotten so far. But each called ahead, and it was indeed okay.

Duncan said that the three men then spent "a wonderful hour together," Sandberg with his guitar, Eisenhower joining in the singing and storytelling.

And that was just one of Duncan MacDougal McDonald Emrich's many stories. What a splendid character.

Va Bene. But not so very.

Languages were always tough for me. Yes, I learned to work, or try to, in German, Italian, Vietnamese, Danish and Norwegian. But except for the Norwegian, all were spoken terribly. I've probably never gotten the grammar correct in a single German sentence. My Vietnamese was minimal: i.e., I used it only if my interlocutors spoke hardly a word of English or French. I'm not a good mimic: both German and Italian have very characteristic sounds, and I couldn't do any of them.

I managed only because I so wanted to, and needed to, communicate. Why else would one want to be in other countries, other cultures? So, for a start, I would begin to speak English like they did ... however they spoke it in that particular land. Coming home with these "foreign accents" caused some amusement: I was asked, more than once, how I liked the U.S. But anyway, I struggled and tried, and folks were patient and forgiving: that we communicated at all was often due much more to my interlocutor's diligence than to my own mutilated efforts. Norwegian and Danish became the only exceptions, and these were actually more "Skandinavisk" — a mixture of Norwegian, Danish and Swedish — than either.

Nevertheless, in each country I took language lessons, did as well as I could, worked in the language when English didn't suffice ...and, when returning to Washington, took the Foreign Service Institute oral exam in whatever language it had been that I'd been garbling.

FSI's language exams involved three people sitting at a table in a little room: the examinee, a native speaker of the language, and a professional linguist. One chatted with the native speaker on subjects suggested by the linguist; one also read and translated articles of increasing difficulty. The grades ran from 0 to 5; five being completely bilingual. "2" was basic "tourist level" and "3" supposedly showed sufficient proficiency to do one's work in the language (to discuss things a press attaché would discuss, for example, but not necessarily be able to explain one's car's problems to a mechanic).

Although I eventually earned a 4+/4+ (the first for speaking, the second for reading and translating) in Norwegian, 3+/4 in Danish and 3/4 in German, I've usually said that my only proven linguistic achievement occurred when I took the Italian exam after my two years in Somalia.

I sat down; we introduced ourselves, and the Senora and I began our conversation. The linguist suggested various topics; I then led the discussion. For some reason, I don't think I ever mentioned that I'd just come from Somalia. And then there was the reading.

Usually one didn't receive one's grade until the next day, but for some reason the linguist told me right away, while still at the table, that my grade would be 2/3: two for speaking, three for reading and translating.

I objected. "I've been doing my job in Italian for the past year."

The rule was that it was the linguist who gave the grade and not the native speaker. But here the Senora burst in, in English:

"Where in the world did you learn such terrible Italian????" she asked, apparently offended to her very core.

"That's irrelevant," I said. "What matters is that I've been doing my job in Italian."

"It sounds as though you learned it from illiterates, who themselves learned it from Siciliani," protested the Senora.

And so I had, in fact; and never had I received such a compliment for my "ear for languages." The Italians who had colonized Somalia were in fact primarily from Sicily: a cynic said that "they were so poor that they couldn't even go to America." And in Somalia they had found folks whom they could look down on. They had used only the "tu" form when addressing Somalis, as one would to children. So most Somalis used only the "tu" form ...and the sort of pidgin Italian which I had apparently learned from them, and with which I have so offended the Senora's Romanesque ears.

"A '3', Sir, is for speaking Italian in Roma! And not in Somalia."

The linguist agreed. But I left a happy man. No one had ever said, of any language that I had ever attempted, that I spoke like a native.

Before All of This

Joining Uncle Sam

It's time to leave exotic Somalia, as I did in April, 1965. But before we get to the next assignment, that in South Vietnam ... how in the world did this character ever become one of our Chosen Abroad????!!!!!

And well you might ask. But in fact, Uncle Sam's diplomatic services are a good deal more diverse ("representative") than many may imagine. There may be time and space later to tell of some of the truly remarkable individuals — virtual national treasures, actually — who have served us as Foreign Service Officers.

But in my own case:

It was a statistical anomaly. As I learned decades later, while serving as deputy executive director of the Board of Examiners for the Foreign Service, the chances of any single individual getting through the months-long hurdles of written exam, oral exam, security and medical clearances, and just plain waiting, are slight indeed. As I recall, in 1980-81, when I was in that role, some 25,000 or so took the annual written exam. Some 2,000 were passed, and were then invited to the day-long oral exam. Some 600 of these were passed ...and of these, perhaps 70 to 150 might, in any one year, actually enter the Foreign Service.

In my case, it probably wouldn't have happened had there not, then, been a separate United States Information Service, independent of the State Department and responsible for press, educational and cultural work. My idiosyncrasies and wanderings and my three years in journalism might not have recommended me as strongly for a more traditional diplomatic role.

It surely would not have happened had John F. Kennedy not been elected President the previous year, and had he not chosen Edward R. Murrow, the nation's foremost journalist, to head USIA. I was well on my way to a journalism career with The Chicago Tribune, or elsewhere, and had numerous and deep reservations about becoming a "propagandist." Murrow's involvement made it almost "okay."

Nor would it have happened had I not, seven years earlier, chosen Antioch College with its work-and-study program, and the on-the-job journalism credentials which I thus had even before graduating; nor without the undergraduate year in Denmark which Antioch had encouraged and enabled.

Finally, I've always suspected that I wouldn't have been chosen to join USIA's Foreign Service had I not lied a bit in my oral exam. I implied that I had spent a night or two in the Greene County, Ohio, jail as a consequence of having protested (which I had actually done) against a discriminating business near the Antioch campus. In most years before and since, jail time would not have been an asset in seeking employment as a diplomat. But that was an unusual time ....

As it happened, I was notified of my acceptance into the Foreign Service on precisely the day that I was also told, at The Chicago Tribune, that my work on the Metro desk had been judged good enough for me to be moved to the City Room ....and thus be embarked on a career in Big City Journalism. But John F. Kennedy, Edward R. Murrow, and visions of a career in Scandinavia decided it ....

Speaking Foreign (as in dansk)

As noted, I was never very good at learning languages, even though I eventually passed the State Department's tests in Norwegian, German and Danish, came close in Swedish, and made heroic efforts in Italian and Vietnamese.

I managed not because I had "the ear," or ever understood the grammar, or could make many of the unique sounds. I managed because I so wanted to communicate: I'd damned well try to understand them, if they'd try to understand me.

At my mother's insistence, I had taken Latin and French in high school, without it having done much good. But when I applied for, and then was accepted for, a year at a Danish folkehøjskole, it was, of course, not expected that one had previous experience with that language.

Instead, the Scandinavian Seminar program sent us all a textbook. And we had language lessons daily on the M/S Kungsholm sailing from New York to Gothenburg. There were more lessons for a week or so in Copenhagen. And then we were sent out to the first of our "host families."

Mine was a young, newly-wed couple living in the tiny hamlet of Ildved in central Jutland. My "mom," Elsabet Sørensen, was, at 23, only two years older than I. Her husband, Einar, was one of two teachers in the village's primary school.

One problem was that the two of them were so very much in love that they hardly even spoke with one another, preferring instead to gaze lovingly into one another's eyes and radiate mutual happiness. I have no idea why they had volunteered to host an American student for a month.

Another problem was that the house that they lived in — "the teacher's house" — was brand new. It lacked carpets, curtains, or anything else to dampen sound.

So we would sit together at a meal — the two of them, seated opposite one another, almost cooing together — and me at the end, terribly conscious of every sound which I was making: my fork striking the plate, my chair creaking, my swallowing unseemly, my stomach gurgling. And every single one of these sounds echoed back and forth from the bare walls.

Of course I was supposed to be using my almost non-existent Danish (the use of English was forbidden, and I have no idea how much of it, if any, they knew). I also had certain needs:

Salt, for example:

A long silence at a mealtime while I try to remember the Danish word for "salt." I finally suspect that it is, in fact, "salt." So I try it:

"SALT, tak," I say, hesitantly. Causing "SALT SALT SALT SALT" to echo between the bare walls.

I have broken their reverie. Seemingly startled, both Einar and

Elsabet look to my end of the table: "Who is THIS??????!!"

I repeat: "Salt, tak." And it echoes again.

Einar reaches the salt cellar and hands it to me.

"Værså go'," he says.

"Tak," say I, vowing never to make this request again. ("And what in the world is 'pepper'?")

But each day I learn a bit more. And I also learn the daily routine. Each afternoon the three of us take a walk through the tiny village. We try to say a few things to each other. They point to things and tell me the word

One afternoon, at walk time, they become unusually vocal. They repeat a number of questions, none of which I understand.

"Forstår du?," they say ("Do you understand?")

"Ja, jeg forstår," I assure them ("Yes, I understand.")

They seem skeptical, but I'm insistent.

We leave for our walk, and get to the hamlet's single cross road just as the daily northbound bus comes through. We board the bus. The bus delivers us to the farm of Elsabet's parents' farm, outside of Horsens. We remain there for a week.

"Strange, this American," I suspect Elsabet was telling her family.

"You would think that he might have wanted to bring his toothbrush, and perhaps a change of clothes ...."

Roskilde Folkehøjskole, 1957-58

Folkehøjskoler — literally "people's high schools", although that's misleading, were, and are, a uniquely Danish (albeit later Scandinavian) institution. They were started in the mid-19th century for at least four reasons: (1) to educate the largely illiterate and impoverished "common folk," the males of whom had been given the vote in 1849; (2) to defend and foster the use of the Danish language (at a time when the Danish elite was increasingly adopting the German language and German cultural norms); (3) to teach women, who would attend the schools in the summer, both literacy and family-raising skills, and (4) teach men, who would attend in the winter, literacy and agricultural skills.

The Danish folkehøjskoler did not, and do not, give either grades or diplomas. "The living word" is emphasized: lectures, song and discussion. There is no professional or vocational training: the goal is to foster communal learning, self-discovery, "enlightenment" and learning how to think. I wonder how many times each week I heard the phrase "broaden your horizons"?

The schools spread rapidly through then-largely-rural Denmark. Each was completely independent: as I recall, the only requirements for the few-questions-asked governmental subsidy was that they teach Danish, and some form of "civics." The early schools, and most still today, promoted a "Christian" (i.e. Danish Lutheran) perspective. But Denmark's Social Democrats, with their unions and the cooperative movement allies, established two folkehøjskoler of their own in the 1920s. One was in Esbjerg, on the west coast; the other was on the Roskildefjord, some 25 miles northwest of Copenhagen.

Someone, in their wisdom, had chosen Roskilde for me, and me for Roskilde. It was serendipitous: one of those happy accidents in one's life, without which one's future could not possibly have evolved as it did. There I learned my first foreign language, without which I could not have joined the Foreign Service. There I fell in love with Scandinavia ... and Scandinavians ... which eventually led to living three-plus years in Norway, two-plus in Denmark, one in Finland, two in Iceland ... and having, for several years, Sweden as my country-in-law. And there Nordic social democracy, and the Nordic welfare states, became my models: what I wanted for my own country, and for others.

There I had also my first head-over-heels love affair. But that's another story.

My roommate at Roskilde was Benny Olsen, a bricklayer from Helsingør. With the exception of the other American student, the lovely Swedish-American Marie Olson, all of our fellow students were skilled or unskilled workers. Some were shop stewards in their unions. The 40 or 45 men averaged perhaps 27 years old; the dozen or so women were younger.

The school's forstander, or headmaster, was Ib Koch-Olsen. Ib was a rarity in the folkehøjskole world: a university-trained individual in an educational movement which, from its earliest history, had prided itself on being quite different from what it perceived as "Latin" academe. Ib had once headed Radio Denmark's cultural division. He was the author of a multi-volume work on Denmark's cultural history. His wife, Gudron Larsen, was a noted sculptor (mostly of cattle!). Her daughter, his step-daughter, became my sweetheart.

An important facet of the folkehøjskole philosophy was that we all lived together on the site: the students, the teachers, the headmaster; the cooks and the janitor, and their spouses and children.

The teacher at my table was Robert Pedersen, later to become a prominent and long-time Social Democratic Member of Parliament and a defense expert who became one of the few voices in his party to defend close U.S. /Danish ties even through the Vietnam war. Robert, like Ib, had a university degree, in economics, but he had earned it in some unorthodox manner, while working as a journeyman typographer. Robert's father had also been a typographer, and a leading Social Democrat in Copenhagen through the 1930's. Early the evening of October 1, 1943, when Robert was 16 or so, he was sent by his father to alert several Jewish families living in central Copenhagen, and celebrating Rosh Hashanah, that they must immediately leave for the basement of a specific hospital in the neighborhood, lest they be rounded up within hours by the occupying Germans. Those who followed the urgent instructions of this young Dane whom they did not know were in the following nights ferried across the sound to Sweden by a flotilla of fishing boats.

"The ones who didn't believe me; which was understandable since there had been little or no antisemitism in Copenhagen, were rounded up and sent to Concentration Camps in Germany. Most died there. The Swedes protected those who reached their shores. They survived," Robert told me.

(You who have visited the Holocaust Museum in Washington, DC, will recall that, following room after room of horrors, there is finally a room celebrating the heroism of individuals who, always at great risk, helped to protect European Jews. Only two whole countries are thanked here. A small Danish fishing boat hangs from the ceiling. Plaques tell the story. The other country celebrated, to the surprise of most, is Bulgaria.)

Robert and Ib were excellent teachers, but the best by far was Daniel Peterson. Daniel was both an able-bodied seaman and a journeyman carpenter. He had sailed the world; visited ports everywhere, and in many countries worked ashore in the building trades. That man could teach geography! The ports! The waterways! The locals! The economies! The geology! The stories. All in the first person. What a teacher!

Forty-plus years later, when heading USIS in our Copenhagen Embassy, I became friends with the rector of Roskilde University. He was, by academic specialty, a geographer. I told him of Daniel and how entrancing he had made geography. "How, Nils," I asked him, "have you folks made geography so dull?" Nils shrugged his shoulders. "That's academe," he said.

Each day started off, after breakfast, with a "morning song"— another century-old folkehøjskole tradition. But instead of hymns, as would have been the case in more traditional folkehøjskoler, our songs were in our "Little Red Song Book." Several of these were proud proletarian anthems, testimonials to labor's struggles in Denmark, elsewhere in Scandinavia, and around the world. One of my favorites — about the only one that I can still sing today — began: "We are the victorious proletariat!; we shall build the happy society." But my fellow students, committed Social Democratic Marxists, were generally quite uncomfortable with songs and perspectives more favored by their traditional competitors in the work place: the Communists. Each May Day there were competing marches through the streets of Copenhagen: one larger and Social Democratic, the other smaller, strident and Communist. My Roskilde bricklayer roommate, Benny, would recall with relish the fist fights with the Communists that he had so looked forward to each May Day.

There were lectures on music, art, history, literature and economics. We did gymnastics. Representatives of each of the national political parties spoke to and with us. On field trips we went into a Swedish coal mine, and to a concert, an art museum, and the raucous seaman's quarter of Copenhagen, Nyhavn.

An important aspect of the Roskilde approach to learning was that we started off with no rules. The group would make them as we went along. Beer was soon outlawed, as were visits by local girls. Folks were to get to class on time. It was to be quiet at night.

I was often in a fog: never entirely sure that I had understood what I was supposed to understand; eventually doing fairly well when the subject was cosmopolitan, but hopelessly lost in gruff, everyday, slang-filled and hastily spoken dialog. I fell seriously in love with Ib's wife's daughter, Elisa. We would sneak fervid minutes together in

Benny's and my room as the evening meal was beginning, arriving at our respective tables a bit late, from opposite entranceways, hoping that no one had noticed.

The maintenance man was a skilled sketcher of landscapes; the headmaster's wife painted the cows in the school's barn; Elisa attended the gymnasium in the town, and the cook took pity on me at Christmas, when everyone else had left (!), and took me home to celebrate the holidays with her family in the unforgettably-named town of Middelfart.

From the school one could see a bit of the Roskilde fjord, the site of many a Viking ship launching. There was a heavy, wet snow fall one day, further embellishing a beautiful hamlet of thatched-roof houses some 20 minutes stroll to the north.

Marie and I followed the Scandinavian Seminar's strict instruction that we two Americans keep apart. Robert, Daniel and Ib would help us with translations if necessary, but otherwise we tried to fit in completely.

"Bob" turned out not to be the most fortuitous name. I learned this one afternoon during perhaps my second week at the school. I had walked into Roskilde, and was now walking home. To my surprise, a woman called to me from a house set back some distance from the sidewalk.

"Bob! Bob!" she called.

I had no idea how this woman knew me — but thought that, as an exotic visiting American, perhaps many did. I opened her gate and headed up a pathway through her garden.

"Bob! Bob! Bob" she called.

"Ja, jeg kommer," I said ("Yes, I'm coming!")

I neared her porch, just a few meters from her.

And then BOB — a white, fluffy, four legged canine Bob — raced to her and jumped into her arms.

"Bob" she cooed, and went inside.

"Bob," it turned out, was, in Denmark, something equivalent to "Fido."

Another inter-cultural lesson learned.

"Fffvvch Hchhq!"

Our Danish school year ended in May 1958. After spending only about $1 per week at school, I had a little bit of money left — at that time one really could wander in Europe for about $5 a day — and set off to see the rest of the Continent.

I stashed my things at the folkehøjskole and set off, hitchhiking. I was to link up with two other Scandinavian Seminar students, one of whom had purchased an old Volkswagen Beatle, at the American Express office in Paris in about a week.

Many young people hitchhiked at that time .. .but of course the girls got picked up much more quickly than the boys. The biggest problem was when getting off the ferries. Twenty or thirty of the passengers might line the exit roads, hoping for a ride with one of the cars pulling off of the ferry. The girls got picked up first, then the lucky fellows ... and those who didn't had to await the next ferry ... and the new female competition that it would also surely bring.

I was picked up by a Dutch fellow on a motor scooter. It was cold, wet, windy and miserable on the back seat of that thing. We crossed over the German border and the weather worsened. We stopped every so often under bridges. I was shivering uncontrollably — but thought, as bedraggled as I was, that I'd never, ever be picked up by anyone else should I abandon my motorcycle buddy.

We overnighted somewhere in Schleswig-Holstein and continued the next morning, in only slightly better weather, into Holland. There, at some point, I got off, and found my way to Amsterdam. I wandered the canals, admired the girls ...and wondered why no one in that country seemed to have heard of a Dutch painter known to all Americans: the man who had famously cut off his ear, Vincent van Gogh.

As one after another Dutch interlocutor admitted to never having heard of the gent, I tried to pronounce his name even more carefully and slowly: "VAN GO." No luck.

Well, I thought, haven't these Europeans done this to any number of great talents in their midst? Mozart? van Gogh? Others? Apparently only we Americans recognized these talents, these geniuses. In their homelands they were so often starved, mistreated, misunderstood, unknown.

Giving up on the Dutch and Van Gogh, I found my way to a highway heading south and was picked up by the driver of a large transport truck. I climbed up into the cab, thanked him, and we chatted. Where was I going? Where had I been? What had I seen? Had I liked Amsterdam?

"Well, yes, I liked Amsterdam," I said. "But I was a bit surprised. There is a Dutch painter who is very famous in America and I had thought there might be some paintings of his here. But no one in Holland seems ever to have heard of him."

"What's his name?" asked the driver.

"Van Go," said I, slowly and carefully.

"Never heard of him," said the driver.

"I know," said I. "No one else has either."

"Write it down," he said.

I did: V A N G O G H.

"Oh!" he said, "Our most famous painter! Fffvvch Hchhq!" And he seemed to gargle and choke ... uttering, it was clear, how "van Gogh" was pronounced in his native tongue.

He loved van Gogh, the driver said. And he felt so badly that I had come all the way to Amsterdam to see his paintings, and hadn't, that he turned the truck around, drove back into the city ... and dropped me off at the elegant national museum which is devoted almost entirely to Vincent Fffvvch Hchhq's work. It was terrific.

Venice ... Maybe

The three of us linked up successfully in Paris and headed, in the old Volkswagen, to the south. We managed on some $5 apiece per day, staying in camping areas (we were invariably the only ones lacking a tent) and living mostly off of bread, cheese and pasta. In a camping area near Genoa we met a South African fellow also traveling without a tent: he joined us in the now quite crowded Beatle.

We checked out the Italian beaches and Rome, and drove over Italy's backbone to the Adriatic coast. We were headed to Venice.

I may have been driving; I may have been the navigator; who knows? In the darkness the road split. We weren't sure how Venice was spelled in Italian, but the road sign seemed to indicate that either fork of the

"Y" would take us there. And it seemed to be a few kilometers closer via the road to the left.

We took it, arrived in Venice, drove around looking for a camping area, and finally followed the signs to one atop a hill. No canals yet, but it was late at night; there would be time for the canals in the morning.

We awoke, enjoyed the view looking down on the town from the hilltop, had our bread-and-cheese breakfast, and drove down to see those famous waterways, gondolas and gondoliers. The town's streets were fairly narrow, and we drove this way and that, a bit surprised that there were not only no canals evident, but no evidence of water either. But it wouldn't be the first time that the Europeans had made much of some sort of sight which, in reality, was much less impressive in fact than it had been in photographs and legend. Maybe this "Venice" was in some corner of the city; maybe it was actually a theme park, with an admission charge.

We happened upon a large black American soldier ambling down a street.

"Hey, Mister, where are the canals in this town?"

"The what?"

"The canals. This town's supposed to be famous for canals. You never saw any?"

"Ah ain't seen no canals here. Never. No how. There may be some. I just ain't seen none myself."

A conference ensued. The map was examined. And there seemed to be both a "Venizia" on the coast, and a "Vicenza" in the hills, some 60 kilometers to the west.. We were, it seemed, in the latter.

So off to the former we headed.

Casino, Signore ...

Three guys do not travel around in a Volkswagen without there being occasional discussions of women, sex, conquests and hunger.

When the three of us post-Denmark Americans joined up with a South African, also in his earliest 20's, he turned out to have Essential Insights that we lacked.

Specifically, that Italy was full of brothels, that they were called

"Casini," and that one obtained directions to them by asking gentlemen in the streets for "Casino, Signore."

Thus it was only a matter of time before the four of us, each feigning considerable savoir faire, set off in search of a Casino, and the pleasures therein.

Glenn, our South African friend, had only one warning for us: that we go to a "high class" Casino ...not a low-end one with diseases and who knew what. With our applicable Italian vocabulary virtually limited to the word "Casino," however, we were going to have to take our chances.

It was evening in one town or another. We noted each individual male on the streets and wondered whether it was he who would conduct us to a brothel. (Although supposedly existent everywhere, they were also supposedly illegal, so it would hardly do to approach a vigilo urbano, a plain clothes policeman, in search of our Casino.)

Eventually we agreed that one individual on a street corner was of the likely sort. Glenn, who had actually been in a casino, was chosen to do the reconnaissance. He went up to the man.

"Casino, Signore?" he said.

"Si," said the man, appraising the four of us. And bade us follow him.

We went down narrow street. We stopped at a large, dark door, and our guide knocked. It opened, we were scrutinized, and invited in. It seemed appropriately "high class": there were rather Victorian furnishings, wallpaper, lamps and so forth. The apparent Madame asked our desires. The negotiating proceeded in Italian, of which we spoke virtually none. But it was pretty apparent why we were there.

Two women, probably in their mid-20's, were invited in. I remember little other than being embarrassed, uncomfortable, about to have my innocence exposed ...and trying my damnedest not to let anyone know. These were rather attractive women ...who wanted which? Or all? Or both? Tutti?????

Someone — perhaps someone also hoping that we'd somehow manage to extricate ourselves from this — asked the price. It was in lira ... perhaps $15.

"Too much," one of us said.

"Troppo."

We others nodded affirmatively. Those two ladies left.

Two others came. Older, seedier, more obviously professional. Now what would our excuse be? Or would, in fact, one or more of us show sufficient manhood to take these, or any other, ladies to the presumed rooms upstairs?

These were about $10. Fumbling, we claimed this was also too much ... hoping, I guess (I had, and have, no idea how the others were perceiving this) that we'd be asked to leave.

But no, there were cheaper wares. Two other "ladies" came in. These were exceedingly hairy, exceedingly whoreish, and perhaps three times our ages. I think they were in the $5 price range; maybe less. At any rate, the price was getting to be such that we could hardly claim that as the excuse for our most unimpressive behavior. Well, the madame had more selections. But, somehow, who knows who began it, the four of us were at the exit door, almost frantic to leave.

Back in the car, the made-up explanations: "God, was she ugly!" "I'd never pay for it ...." "My girlfriend ... I couldn't risk giving her something." And so forth. Four innocents abroad, even post-Casino.

Aspiring Expatriate

Our $5 per day Volkswagen "grand tour" proceeded from Venice through Trieste and Ljubljana to Vienna, and thence to Salzburg and Munich. We would be splitting up in Munich, and I had no plans at that point ... nor any reservations to get back home. I thought that perhaps I wouldn't go back to the U.S. at all ... I would be an expatriate; I would live like Hemingway and others. In Paris, in Spain, on the Riviera. But how?

Before leaving Denmark I had written to Antioch, to the office which found co-op jobs for us, asking for any suggestions. Awaiting me at the American Express mail slot in Munich was a reply. It suggested that I contact the Carl Duisberg Gesellshaft in Cologne. They found jobs in German industry, mostly for Third World workers ... but perhaps they'd have work for me, as well.

Glenn, our new South African buddy, was also all but out of money. He would come to Cologne with me; perhaps we would both find jobs.

We hitchhiked to Cologne, and found the office of the Carl Duisburg Gesellshaft. Yes, they knew about Antioch. They'd never placed an American student in a German factory job so I would be the first. I was to go to a factory in an industrial suburb of Düsseldorf and speak with the foreman there. Glenn could try, too.

We went, and were hired. I immediately presented a problem, though: I would need a cash advance so that I could go back to Denmark to fetch the items that I'd left there. This was approved, and I left.

But it wasn't my things that I was so desperate to return to Roskilde for: it was Elisa, my heartthrob, my sweetheart, the girl of all of my dreams; my Nordic Goddess; she who encapsulated all that I loved about Denmark, the North, and this new world; she whom I was crazy about; she who had sent delicious letters to me at the several American Express offices; she whom I would surely, probably now, ask to be my wife.

I was grubby when I left Cologne, and grubbier still when I arrived, this time by train, at the Roskilde train station. I would take the bus to a camping area farther up the fjord, beyond the school (where Elisa, the daughter of the headmaster, lived). I would shower, sleep, shower, look my best ...and go to see, and surprise, my sweetie.

Bushed and beat and grungy, I piled into the bus ...and encountered Elisa: clean, gorgeous, delicious, surprised. And quite matter-of-fact. I sat down next to her.

By the time the bus arrived at the school, ten minutes later, I had been told that ("strange, isn't it, so sudden?") Elisa had "fallen out of love" with me, wasn't in love with me at all any more, that it was all over ... and that I really didn't need to go to the trouble of seeing her again while I was in town.

Devastation.

And very probably the reason that, for almost all of the rest of my life, it was I who ended relationships.

"I just don't love you anymore," she had shrugged.

Elisa! Let me shower! Let me rest! Let me wash up! Let me bring flowers!!!!!!!!!!!!!!! Let me start all over again! WHY?????????!!! But it was too late, over. And the only reason to be in Denmark at all now; to be anywhere, was to pick up my suitcase of stuff. And to be off, Elisa-less, for the rest of my life.

Expatriate Proletarian

So I returned to Düsseldorf, sooner than expected, and heartbroken.

Glenn had started work already, cutting huge rolls of sandpaper into little squares for some nine hours per day, and was glad to have company. He was living in a dormitory in a home for gastarbeiter, "guest workers" in Germany. It was cheap and included food. But I wasn't ready to be sharing quarters in bunkbeds; I needed to nurse my melancholy alone. I took a room at the YMCA: a mistake, it turned out, since it, plus my meager daily food, plus the trolley fare to the factory and back, cost absolutely every pfennig of my meager wages (from which the advance for my Denmark trip was being deducted).

This was the summer of 1958, the beginning of the German "economic miracle." But much of it was based on very cheap labor, both from East Germany and from the Third World. Later, when German wages became the world's highest, and its benefits among the world's best, it would be hard to recall that, in the late 1950's, labor had been cheaper than machines.

My job was to cut sandpaper, using the same type of single-bladed, manually-operated cutter that one used in school art classes (or today in Staples), to cut long strips of sand paper into pieces about 5 x 5 inches, and pile them in stacks of 100. We wrapped each pile with string, and put them onto a cart for shipping out to hardware stores across the land.

Glenn and I shared a paper cutter. One of us advanced the roll the requisite distance, then pulled the cutter blade. This was a standing job.

The other sat, counted, and kept the little piles orderly. This person also tied the finished piles with string.

What could change from hour to hour ... the only thing that could change ...was the language in which we counted. We did English, German, Danish, French, Zulu and Afrikaans. One could also count backwards.

Extremely short visits to the toilet were permitted, but barely. There was a checker who noted how long any one pair of feet had been in the stall. A moment too long, and one's pay was docked one-half hour. Similarly, if the trolley arrived even a minute late in the morning, another half-hour of pay was gone. There was a half-hour lunch break. We brought our own sandwiches. And said "Mahlzeit" to one another.

I had just finished a year at a Social Democratic, union-run school in Social Democratic heaven: Denmark. And here I was in my first proletarian job: an assembly line. Surely everyone here was a Social Democrat, a union member?

Hardly any, as it turned out. Most if not all of the factory's workers had come from East Germany (this was before the Wall, so one can't really say they had "fled," but they had made a clear choice). After their experiences in Communist East Germany, they were suspicious of, and almost instinctively against, anything "leftist"; anything "social", maybe even anything supposedly for "workers." They were Adenauer, CDU folks, one and all.

Besides, one told me at lunch one day, "they say that the head of the Social Democratic party in Düsseldorf is a Jew."

So I, surely the only college-educated individual on the factory's work force, was seemingly also its only pro-union, pro-Social Democratic individual.

I was called into the foreman's office one morning. What had I been saying to the red-headed girl named Olga?

"Nothing, I think," I said ... the foreman being, aside from Glenn, the only person in the plant to whom I could speak English.

"Nothing? Not at lunchtime?" he asked.

"Well, I guess we joked a bit," I said.

"Did you tell her that you wanted to marry her and take her to America?"

"Well, I guess I may have joked about that."

"Please, Herr Dickerman, bitte bitte. Do not joke with us Germans. Olga has told me she is quitting her job to marry you and go to America. And now she does not understand why you have been behaving differently."

Nor would it be the last time that I was told not to presume that what I might think funny would be taken as such by Germans.

A bit of humor (and/or silliness) had worked pretty well in Denmark. But not here.

Going Home

After a couple of months of cutting sandpaper, moping in my YMCA room, and having barely enough money to eat, life as an expatriate was seeming less and less attractive. Perhaps Hemingway had approached it differently.

But without Elisa, without food and without friends other than Glenn, Europe was losing its charm. I might as well go home, go back to the newspaper in Battle Creek; start my senior year at Antioch.

I don't recall asking my mother for the money for the ship back home, but I must have. Or perhaps it was saved somewhere, since I must have realized when beginning the year in Denmark that I'd be going back sometime?

In any case, I went to a travel agent in Düsseldorf and paid for a steerage-class fare on a ship that would be departing from Bremerhaven in two or three weeks. But I had hardly any other money, and they would be subtracting, from my last paycheck at the sandpaper factory, what remained of my earlier advance.

I hitchhiked out of Düsseldorf for Bremen, going without food for a day or so, and asked directions to my ship. But Bremen's harbor, Bremerhaven turned out to be quite a different place, some 40 kilometers away ...and hours of futile thumb-wagging for a grungy, hungry, hollow-eyed hitchhiker. I finally arrived at the pier, and was told that there would be no boarding until the next afternoon. Another night on a park bench; another 24 hours without food. This was not the expatriate life that I had envisioned.

I was at the head of the line the next afternoon, famished and exhausted, when the gangway was finally opened. My ticket was checked, I was told my room number, and pointed in the direction of the canteen, where I would be assigned seating and a meal time.

They assigned me to the second seating, and I imploded.

"No! You can't do this to me! I haven't eaten for three days! Please! Please!!!!!!!!!!!! Please! Help me!"

And it was changed.

Rarely has a buffet table been attacked with such alacrity and purpose.

I was out on the deck again as we pulled away. A band played "Auf Wiedersehen." I thought it was the saddest song I had ever heard.

And I was sure that I would never see Europe again. I went back to Battle Creek, worked a few weeks on the local paper, finished my senior year at Antioch, graduated ...and spent the summer working on my dad's farm in the Shenandoah Valley until my next incarnation, as an aspiring Air Force officer (yep) would begin.

Failed Warrior

When I'd been yanked from my Finnish paradise to desolate Somalia, it had been, I was told, because, with so many African countries becoming independent, and so many Embassies opening in them, that I (and we) were "needed." But there was supposedly going to be a reward for this: possibly a return to Europe ...or at least something like Marrakesh. But those sleazy salesmen of Foreign Service postings in 1963 hadn't anticipated what the American buildup in South Vietnam in 1965 would require. Now, I was told, Uncle Sam really did need me.

"And if you have problems with this, Bob, you can go right down the hallway and resign. This afternoon."

So once again, "principles" gave way to mushiness. Young Dickerman, the one-time president of the Antioch Pacifist Club, was going off to war. Just as, six years earlier, a few months after his college graduation, he had become a member of the first co-educational officer training class in the United States Air Force.

That two-month stint had worked out rather weirdly:

It was really not the lifestyle that I preferred.

It was pretty awful.

We marched. We stood at attention. We saluted. Our socks, our underwear, and everything else had to be placed absolutely as absurdly required in our drawers and lockers. Our beds had to be made in a certain way.

It was awful.

There were at least three weekends when no one in my unit was permitted to go into San Antonio ... all because of my socks, or underwear, or some such.

I was not particularly popular.

There were perhaps 50 individuals in this first-ever class of the first-ever "Officer Training School" at Lackland Air Force Base. This was back in the time of the Draft. Few of us males would have been in the military otherwise: it was either this, or being enlisted men.

But there were also a dozen or so women in the class. None of them had to be there: every single one of them was there by choice: bloodthirsty, horrible, unwomanly, unhuman! creatures in my humble judgment.

I hated that place; was miserable, and thought the gung-ho attitude of these women absolutely atrocious.

When we ate, we couldn't choose where to sit. It had to be the next empty place. And when we ate, it was as "square meals": no talking; fork raised vertically, then a 90 degree turn into the mouth.

The individual at the head of each table had to march that group of "troops" back to their quarters.

I found myself, one awful evening, at the head of a table of these ladies.

I contemplated marching them home.

A foolishly immature recent liberal arts graduate, I was sure that I knew exactly why we spent so much time marching: it was, I knew; I had read; to beat us into obeying commands without thinking for ourselves.

It was a cold, wet, rainy, dreary evening when I assembled my ladies outside for the march home.

I had to test my theory: had they been turned into robots, obeying any order ... or did they still have a brain of their own????

We came to a "T" intersection. There were two commands I could have given: one would turn the "column" 90 degrees. The other would have been to order two 45 degree turns, one right after the other.

I gave the first 45 degree order, but not the second. And the ladies — I could hardly believe it! — marched over the side of the road, slid down an embankment, and finally stopped ankle-deep in mud.

Incredible.

But a car came by, its driver slamming on the brakes. A large, ruddy-faced colonel got out, yanking his "gig book" out of his shirt pocket. (On this training base, all officers carried these.) I suppose, looking back at it, that he was probably a careerist horrified that women were now joining his beloved Air Force.

He was set to gig every one of my ladies.

"Sir," I said. "It's not their fault. I didn't give the second order."

His jaw dropped. And he gave me what I knew to be a Major, Major, Major Gig.

Back in my barracks, I showed it to my lieutenant.

"You will be sent to Leavenworth," he said. "You may be executed."

But even he was surprised when, the next morning, I was ordered to report to the Commanding Officer of Lackland Air Force Base.

"You really are in trouble, Dickerman," the lieutenant said.

I marched to the Commanding General's building. Up the stairs. And was shown into his office.

Now one doesn't, in this situation, say "Hi, General," and shake hands, then sit down:

"Officer Trainee Dickerman, Charles R., Number Whateveritwas, reporting as ordered, SIR!" I said, trying to click my heels in the most proper and Nazi-like manner.

The general, behind his large desk, stared at me for several of the longest moments of my life. I was sure that I WAS going to be executed.

"Dickerman," he finally said, "this Air Force needs men like you!!!!!"

Absolutely stunned, I managed a weak: "Yessir. But why Sir????"

"Because this Air Force is full of men who never take responsibility. You did a Goddamned stupid thing. You admitted it. Most wouldn't. We need men like you, Dickerman.

"That's all," he said.

I saluted, wheeled, clicked, marched out of his office, down the corridor, down the stairs, out onto the parade grounds.

"This is even worse," I thought. "Now they'll probably never let me out."

But they did, only a few weeks later. And I lived to tell the story. And eventually to serve, as a civilian, TWO years in Vietnam ... while few in the military served more than one.

But now for a real war ....

South Vietnam, 1965-67

Welcome to a Scary Place

Somewhere along the line, in my mid-20's, I think, I had gotten the idea … the firm conviction, actually … that I would not live to see my 30th birthday. Thus, when I finally acquiesced, after much worry, complaints and shenanigans, to being assigned to Vietnam, I was virtually certain that I knew where the end would come. I was 28 years and nine months old when I arrived in that scary place. I was sure, therefore, that I was then living out — in a place I definitely did not want to be — the last 15 months, the last 450 days or so, of my life. Believing this makes every day scary. And each day that passed increased the odds that the next day might be "it." I never wrote a letter from Vietnam without thinking that it might be the last that the recipient(s) might ever hear from me. Each letter was thus determinedly cheerful, conveying the Bob that I'd want them to remember.

"It really is remarkable," my dad once wrote, "with so much going on elsewhere in Vietnam, that you seem to be in such a safe and pleasant spot."

My life and work in the Vietnamese Delta, in the Mekong Delta west and southwest of Saigon, was indeed safer and pleasanter than that of many Americans there. But things were decidedly less safe and pleasant than was the situation of thousands of Americans in Saigon … including our bosses. Out in the provinces, things blew up. Mines went off. Rounds sometimes came in. Co-workers were killed. Vietnamese in the area were dying by the hundreds.

But although, for us "field representatives," Saigon came to be viewed as a haven of luxurious housing, good dining and great raunchiness, I experienced my first hours there as War, Danger, Fright and Concern. Lyndon Johnson had sent me to help the good Vietnamese beat the bad ones. I had never been in Asia before, nor in a war. I'd had some eight weeks of Vietnamese language training. The only guns I'd ever shot were a .22 rifle and a .12 gauge shotgun. The only things I'd ever shot were cans, squirrels and rabbits. And no one had ever shot at me.

And how was anyone who might be inclined to shoot at me to know that I was not Lyndon Johnson, not General Westmoreland, not a warrior ... and not even sure that what we were doing in that troubled place was right?????

"Hey, wait, don't shoot! I'm Bob Dickerman, boy liberal; onetime president of the Antioch Pacifist Club; I didn't want to come here at all!" But that probably wouldn't work. And how would one say it in Vietnamese, anyway?????

I had arrived just in time for a semi-annual meeting in Saigon of all of the "field representatives" of my new organization, the Joint United States Public Affairs Office, or JUSPAO. JUSPAO's job was to "win the hearts & minds (WHAM!)"; we were the "pyschwarriors," the psychological warfare guys. Nor was JUSPAO's focus only on influencing the Vietnamese. It was also JUSPAO that hosted the "five o'clock follies": the daily media briefings for the American and world press; Uncle Sam's daily effort to demonstrate how splendidly well things were "working."

I remember nothing of our meetings that first day, except that I was always on alert for something to go "boom" or "bang." I read the leaflets which we received on "personal safety," and reviewed them again when heading to bed in the downtown "bachelor officer quarters" hotel in which we were billeted. There had been a number of recent bombings of these and other U.S. facilities in Saigon. Sometimes the bombs were in pairs: the second bigger than the first, and killing those who had come to help with, or just to see, the damage of the first.

Sometime during that first night there was a terrific blast. The building shook, and glass seemed to be falling forever, as it landed on the sidewalk, in rapid succession, from the windows of each higher story of the building.

I grabbed my pillow, as the leaflet had instructed, and put it over my head. But my roommate, who had been "field repping" for several months in dangerous Pleiku in the Central Highlands, was sleepily groping his way to the now shattered window.

"Jim! Goddamn it! Get down! There could be another one!" I shouted.

"Some bastard's throwing beer bottles down there," he mumbled. "SHUT UP DOWN THERE!"

What in the world must Pleiku be like, I wondered, if something like that sounds like busting beer bottles.

Several months later, at home in My Tho, I awoke one morning to a bedroom even more disheveled than usual. Window glass was all over the floor; hung pictures had fallen from the walls. I had finally learned to sleep in spite of the all-night shooting of out-going mortar rounds during my weekly stays in my more dangerous province to the north, but clearly what had happened in My Tho during my sleep was something unusual.

At the military's briefing that morning I learned what had happened: a ship, anchored in the Mekong two blocks from the house, had been blown up. And I hadn't even thought that beer bottles were being broken.

"Mr. Dickerman: What is the Answer????"

I had arrived in South Vietnam in the late summer of 1965, part of that year's huge escalation of American military and civilian personnel. We'd been increasing the number of "advisors" since the mid-50s. But things had not been improving: to the contrary; as would be repeated through two decades, Washington's assessment was that improvement, and "victory," required more Americans on the ground, more Americans doing the fighting ourselves; more American military and civilian advisors at ever lower levels of the Vietnamese infrastructure.

Some of us may actually have arrived with something useful to impart. And most of us certainly tried to do our best. But many must have been as ill-prepared and poorly qualified as I:

Before arriving in Saigon I had spent exactly one previous night in

Asia — and that had been in Tokyo en route there. I'd never been in a war zone before. I'd had some eight weeks of Vietnamese language training, but that was practically worthless. What I knew of Vietnam — its history, its culture, its language, its geography, its rancor — was minimal (but, I should say, was more than most military personnel had acquired).

I'd shot a .22 rifle and a .410 shotgun when hunting with my dad. In Saigon I was issued a pistol and an M-1 semi-automatic weapon, without instruction as to their use or their maintenance. I was 28 years old, and scared to death.

The drive from Saigon to my new hometown of MyTho took a couple of hours. Someone drove the Scout; Don Beesom and I sat on the tailgate, weapons at the ready (I tried to guess: How does this damned thing work?????)

I was introduced to Mr. Hiep, who would be my close colleague for the duration of my tour. Mr. Hiep took me to my new home: a tidy single story four room bungalow with a detached kitchen, one block from the hospital of the Vietnamese 7th Infantry Division, and two blocks from the mighty Mekong River.

The next morning Mr. Hiep took me down the street to meet my local counterpart: Mr. Hoa, the director of the Vietnamese Information Service in Dinh Tuong province (of which My Tho was the administrative headquarters).

And there I realized what a responsibility Mr. Hoa thought I had; how much wisdom he believed I had to impart.

"We will do everything you tell us to do," Mr. Hoa said. "You are very wise. That is why you have been sent to us."

I? Wise? Mr. Hoa was perhaps 20 years older than me. He could hardly remember a time of peace. He knew where places were and who was who. He knew the province's history. He had seen much that didn't work, and some that did. But like thousands of his compatriots at the time, he believed — he wanted to believe; he had been told to believe — that Uncle Sam had the answers.

Uncle Sam in the person of ... me.

"I have gotten you a cook and housekeeper," Mr. Hoa said. 'You will be happy here."

When I returned home late that afternoon, this "cook and housekeeper" was already there. Although I did not yet have any experience with Saigon's "bar girls," this lady's appearance, demeanor, GI English and high heels more than suggested that she was an alumna of that profession, and a well-worn one at that.

We told Mr. Hoa the next morning that this particular choice was not going to work; that I really did want a cook and a housekeeper ... and would he please try again.

That evening when I went home the new lady was present. She was certainly not a city girl, nor a girl at all, but a very peasanty woman from the countryside.

Ron Robichaud, my counterpart with USAID, had come home with me. We asked madame to please bring us "deux bières" (my pidgin French) ..."hai loại bia" (in Ron's more practiced Vietnamese).

The lady shuffled, barefoot, to the kitchen, returned with two cans and squatted on the living room floor, manipulating a screwdriver as a can opener.

Ron and I watched with fascination, wondering what her reaction would be when she found the contents of the cans to be not beer, but beans.

So we freed Mr. Hao of this self-imposed obligation, and Mr. Hiep found the wonderful Madame Nga. Madame Nga, whose two youngest of 12 children sometimes came to the house with her, remained with me through my tour. So, like so many others with whom I then dealt, she paid a high price when the Viet Cong cadres took over the city in May 1975.

Elephant Grass

I was not only scared in Vietnam, but very lonely. There was no one with whom I could share what I was thinking and feeling. That I was a "psychwarrior," that I knew anything about what was going on or what should be done, was a daily charade. I've never been comfortable dealing with the military, and was doing so constantly there: with the MAC/V advisors in My Tho, with the Special Forces units in Moc Hoa, and with the local Vietnamese 7th Division commanders. I hated being there, and what I was doing. Both the "Viet Cong" and the Saigon government were nasty; it obviously was, in the Delta at least, a civil war and not a war of North Vietnamese aggression.

What motivation I conjured drew from several perceptions: (1) there was more hope that a "decent" Vietnamese citizen might have some influence within the South Vietnamese system than that of the National Liberation Front; (2) we had leverage with the Government side, and some of the things that we were doing were certainly justified, needed and desirable; (3) perhaps those who had made the decisions in Washington that had sent me and a half-million other Americans to Vietnam actually knew what they were doing (a hope that dimmed as time passed) and most importantly: (4) I came to know a half dozen truly sterling Vietnamese individuals, folks who were "doing good" in spite of every disincentive and danger. Such individuals ...I considered them Social Democrats ...men and women wanting both democratic rule and economic justice. Such individuals were threats to both sides. But they could at least work and set examples on "our" side.

I had no friends, really, although Huynh-thi-Tri, one of the most admirable people I've ever known, became one eventually. And so, as during so many other times in my life, I fantasized an alternative: Scandinavia. And finally, one of those denizens arrived in my doorstep in My Tho.

He was Nils Morten Udgaard, a reporter with Oslo's principal paper, Aftenposten. Convinced that the story we had to tell was better than what people were seeing, hearing, reading and imagining around the world, Uncle Sam was paying the tickets for hundreds of hand-picked journalists, from around the world, to come to South Vietnam to see it for themselves.

Nils Morten was about my age, late 20's; a fine fellow, and we later became good friends when, after Vietnam, I was sent as press attaché to Paradise ... oops, Norway. But we met for the first time there at my house in My Tho.

He stayed overnight, and the next day we went, as he wished, "on an operation." This was an operation by the Vietnamese "popular forces", the local militias. We boarded a truck, headed somewhere. I had never been on such an operation before ...or any military operation ... but didn't reveal it. I was also scared, but tried not to reveal that either.

In any case, as with so many ... all but a few, actually ... of South Vietnamese military operations, we encountered no one, and returned to the town safely, well before sunset. (Few if any of us would have dared to venture, even with more firepower, into that area after dark.)

After supper, Nils Morten put his typewriter on the table and began his story for Aftenposten. After a while, I came up and looked over his shoulder at his copy:

"Da vi gikk gjennom elefantgræsset ..." his lead read. "As we went through the elephant grass ...."

"Nils Morten," I said. "There's no elephant grass here in the Delta. Elephant grass is in Central Vietnam."

"Aftenposten's readers expect there to be elephant grass here," said my new friend. "And so it is." And he continued pecking out his report.

This seemed to me for years to characterize not only much reporting from the Vietnam war, but much reporting of, well, everything. "The readers expect there to be (fill in the blank) here, and so it is."

Nils Morten Udgaard went on to a distinguished Norwegian journalism career. He was Aftenposten's bureau chief in Bonn, Washington, London and Moscow, as well as its foreign editor in Oslo. But only he knew why I persisted him in calling him "Elefant Græs Udgaard."

I'd Rather be at the Dentist's

The fear continued. I wasn't being put into harm's way, as were soldiers. And I certainly wasn't tempting trouble, as did some. But death in Vietnam couldn't be predicted. I hated driving the roads, and had so many sandbags on the floor on my International Scout that the brakes would give out. I carried both an M-1 semi-automatic rifle and a pistol (some sort of six shooter). I'd never fired either but kept both fully loaded. I never cleaned them, and perhaps they wouldn't even have worked. And I had some concern that the rifle, which I would have aimed with my left eye, being left-handed, would rapidly expel the spent shells right into my other eye. And probably I was a more tempting target just because I had the weapons, than I would have been without. In any case, I had them with me everywhere, except in the city of My Tho, where I lived and spent four or five days each week.

I knew very little about guns, anyway. A Special Forces soldier in Moc Hoa, noticing that I actually had six rounds in the chamber of my six-shooter, warned me against it. The pistol had in fact fallen out of its holster on more than one occasion. "If it lands on the hammer, buddy, you could be shot right in the balls," he said.

And once I had removed the pistol from the holster of the Vietnamese policeman who, assigned to guard my house, usually fell asleep in a chair on the porch. I doubted that there was actually much danger there at home, and knew that the cop, or his family, must have bribed someone significantly to be assigned such easy and safe duty. But still, it seemed to me, he should at least look as though he was awake, alert and ready.

So, as he snored, I unsnapped his holster, took his pistol, and delivered it to the Chief of Police. My guard, upon awakening, would have some explaining to do. Not surprisingly, I never saw him again. And his successors seemed somewhat more alert.

"But that was stupid," said an old CIA hand. "People who are trained in weapons don't have to be wide awake to use them. You're damned lucky he didn't blow a hole right through you."

This was not the kind of Foreign Service living that I thought myself especially good at: relishing the breezes and beauties of Scandinavia, or perhaps a bucolic university town. But the clock was ticking, and there were fewer and fewer days remaining until I would (not) be 30.

The Viet Cong controlled all but the principal roads through the Delta, and even on those they would sometimes put up road blocks, demand "taxes" of passing vehicles ... and kill or capture "enemies." An American civilian would have been crazy to be on any road at all in the evening or early morning; nighttime travel would be unthinkable. Nor would Vietnamese civilians who had some connection with the Saigon government, even schoolteachers, be much safer.

I was once driving later than I should have from Saigon to My Tho when, about halfway down, I came upon a long line of stopped Vietnamese vehicles.

Should I stop? Was it a roadblock? Should I turn around? Dare I ask anyone what's going on?

For whatever combination of reasons (and fear), I decided it was too dangerous to stop, turn, or ask. I was apparently the only American there: who knew what could happen? I barreled down the road as fast as I could drive, rushing past some pretty astonished, patiently waiting, Vietnamese. I had seen in a "personal safety" film that one might plow through a simple roadblock, throwing both barriers and people aside in one's wake.

But there wasn't a roadblock, "only" a firefight: guys on each side of the raised road firing at their enemies on the opposite side. And here comes a big white International Scout barreling right between them.

Who knows what they thought. The Scout took a couple of rounds on both sides, but I could hardly take it personally. I'd been a damned fool. And now there was one less day until I would (not) reach 30. "If I ever do get out of here," I said to myself, "I'll never, ever complain in a dentist's chair again. I'll just think about how much rather I'd be there than any road here in Vietnam." And I have. And many a dentist has been amazed.

My Window into Vietnam: Huynh-thi-Tri

That I didn't die by age 30, and there in South Vietnam, I ascribed to three things: (1) my cowardice (read "caution" if you will; I took no chances there that I didn't have to take) (2) the protective guidance of my Vietnamese colleague, Mr. Hiep; and (3) most of all, the friendship of Ms Huynh-thi-Tri.

Ms Tri (Co Tri in Vietnamese) taught in the girls' secondary school in My Tho. She lived with her mother, sister and brother near the town center, a few blocks from my home. She was beloved of her students and highly respected in the community. Still in her late 20's, she was an inspiration and mentor to many.

I first learned of Ms Tri when my counterpart from the U.S. Agency for International Development (USAID), Ron Robichaud, nominated her for a six-month grant to study social work in the U.S. . Ron had been impressed by the efforts of her students to help improve the lot of the city's poor. In a society in which, quite understandably, most people were concerned only for their own safety and welfare, Tri led her students into the poor hamlets on the edge of town to provide help and encouragement. She helped the Buddhist nuns in their pathetic orphanage, where as many as three or four often-dehydrated infants lay in a single crib. She encouraged her students to visit the wounded soldiers in the military hospital a few steps from my home. And just as she inspired her students, her example gave the American "advisors" reason to believe, in spite of ample evidence to the contrary, that the country was not comprised only of communist guerrillas and corrupt government officials, but also of many who deserved, and would struggle for, better lives than either side in this long, awful war would provide them. I considered her, and still do, the most admirable person I had ever known.

When the Saigon regime collapsed in 1975, Tri would pay a heavy price for her support of grassroots cooperation between the local people and Americans both civilian and military. She was first in a "re-education center" where, married and pregnant, she nearly died. This was followed by years of house arrest and surveillance. Not until the early 80's was she permitted to re-unite with her husband, Toan, who had had his own re-education camp and house arrest experiences. With two children, the family's prayer was to qualify for the U.S.' "orderly departure program." In the interim, every time they found a way to support themselves — harvesting wild honey, re-bagging rice, making wooden toys — the cadre shut them down. Their son Tuan was on a school swimming team. When he made known his intention to quit swimming and study English instead, the cadre said his "extra" weekly food ration would be stopped. The family endured heartbreak after heartbreak as their applications for the Orderly Departure Program were variously delayed, lost, delayed, lost, and finally rejected outright.

If I needed some sort of supernatural explanation for my Foreign Service career having dismayingly come to an end in Copenhagen at age 56, it would be that this was what put me back in Washington just at the time Tri's family most needed me. By a serendipitous (as in Buddha-guided???) series of coincidences, I was able to review their huge file and to find that they had, in fact, earlier been approved. Three members of Congress, California's Nancy Pelosi, Minnesota's Gerry Sikorski and Virginia's Rick Boucher — all of whom had constituents who wrote of their high regard for Tri — co-signed a letter to the Immigration and Naturalization Service asking that they be granted "humanitarian parole."

A few months later, in mid-1993, Tri, husband Toan, daughter Maivan and son Tuan Son, arrived in Pinehurst, NC, to live with their sponsor Katherine Clarkin Klein.

Katherine always wanted me to "write a book" about Tri — who, we agreed, seemed, like high quality steel, to have gained great strength from pressures which crushed so many others. Katherine saved all of Tri's correspondence and notes, as did I. Daughter Maivan now has them. Suffice it here to say that both children are now married and parents themselves, working hard, living "the American dream," and contributing very usefully to their communities of Pinehurst and Durham, North Carolina.

A Democratic Home

As in virtually all of America's wars, we claimed in South Vietnam to be defending democracy ...or at least incubating it. But the Republic of Vietnam's government was in no way democratic ... although it permitted, certainly, more diversity of views, and more diversity of endeavors, than did communist North Vietnam.

In any case, we needed to appear to be supporting democratic self-government in South Vietnam, and I don't doubt for a moment but that the vast majority of Vietnamese, living under any of the three regimes (Republic of Vietnam, Democratic Republic of Vietnam and the National Liberation Front) aspired to such a state.

In 1968 it was decided (probably in Washington) that the first step toward making South Vietnam into a democratic society would be to create a Constitution. Wheels spun and papers were issued: each province was to elect citizens who would go to Saigon, form a Constitutional Convention, and draft the nation's new basic law.

In Dinh Tuong, with some 600,000 people my "big" province, seven men declared themselves candidates for the assembly. They included, as I recall, two military officers, two refugees from North Vietnam, a lawyer, a businessman ... and a favorite of mine, Mr. Tuc.

Mr. Tuc was truly a "man of the people": a humble, unpretentious man — qualities which already distinguished him from the other six candidates. I had met him through my schoolteacher friend, Miss

Tri. The two of them shared a commitment to bettering the lot of ordinary folk.

Mr. Tuc was an elected officer of the local union of transport workers: the men who brought produce to the market by either bicycle cart or vehicle. He was a familiar face at the My Tho peasants' market. His union was a part of the nationwide labor confederation, the CVT, La Confederation Vietnamienne du Travail.

The CVT was, I think, the single nationwide democratic institution in South Vietnam. Formed during the French colonial regime and modeled after the industrial unions of France proper, it worked hard and effectively on behalf of its some 550,000 members. From the local branches to the national confederation, its leaders were elected for set periods, and then had to stand for election again.

Mr. Tuc was thus the only candidate of the seven who had actual experience in a democratic organization.

Following rules that evidently had come down from Saigon, the seven candidates were brought together at several events where they could speak to, and be seen by, the voters. These events had to be secured, of course, and the peasants attending them probably had little choice but to be there.

I attended one of these events, held late one afternoon in a school in a village a few kilometers from My Tho, on the highway to Saigon. The peasants, all in their "black pajamas," sat uncomfortably in rows; the seven candidates for the Constitutional Assembly were at a table in the front. The moderator was, I believe, the deputy province chief, a civilian. My Vietnamese colleague, Mr. Hiep, gave me brief summaries of what was being said.

Eventually there was a question for Mr. Tuc. An elderly peasant woman with a deeply lined face and rounded shoulders said this, basically:

"Tuc ...we know you are a very good man. You are an honest man. You do much to try to help the people. We have known you for many years. We love you.

"But Tuc, these other men are educated: they are lawyers, and professors, and learned men. You have no education, Tuc; you are like us. Why should we vote for you, Tuc, instead of these wise men?"

Mr. Tuc responded with what I have since often described as the most beautiful description of Constitutional governance that I have ever heard:

"Thank you, Madame. You are right. These honorable men are very wise. They are very educated. I am just a simple worker. I have no education.

"But when a family builds its home, it needs many different specialists.

"It needs a mason to lay the floor. It needs a carpenter to erect the building. It needs a roofer to lay the roof. It may need a plumber to bring in the pipes. It needs many specialists who have learned their trades so that they can do it well.

"Each of these is very important.

"But the most important person that the family needs is the architect. The architect must know the family. He must know the family well. Only if he knows the family well can he design the house to bring harmony and happiness to the family. That is why the architect is so important.

"My friends: the Constitution that we are going to write in Saigon will be the house of our people. It will be our home. Yes, to write it we will need experts. We will need lawyers. And professors.

"But the most important is the architect. The architects must understand the people so that the house which we design will be one in which our Vietnamese family can live in harmony and happiness.

"That is why it is very, very important that we send to Saigon, to the Constitutional Assembly, men who understand our people, who understand what we need in our new house, our new home.

"When we go to Saigon, we can call the experts. We can call the lawyers, and the professors. We will need their help. But they are perhaps not the best architects ...."

Mr. Tuc lost. Or actually, I think, he was disqualified. Mr. Tuc's work as a produce driver took him daily from town into the outlying rural areas. Anyone who had such work had been stopped at road blocks set up by the Viet Cong/National Liberation Front. Anyone who had such work had paid the "taxes" collected at these road blocks. And anyone who was as honest as Mr. Tuc admitted this.

His admission was the grounds for his disqualification. The lawyers, the professor, the military officers who were running either had never had this basic, continuing experience of Vietnamese life ... or lied about it. One or another of them was elected. The new Constitutional home of the Vietnamese people was never erected.

A Second K.I.A: Tran-Doan-Cam

I'll find it eventually. If there was to be one heart-stopper among these tales, it would have been the text of that neatly hand-written letter, in English, delivered to me one morning in My Tho, from Tran-Doan-Cam. I came across it several years ago when going through old papers. As soon as I realized what it was, I pushed it away. I still couldn't bear to re-read it. But I know that I kept it. I just can't figure out where.

My Field Representative's "black bag" of Uncle Sam's money had enabled me to pay Mr. Cam, who was in his early 20's, to do what was very much needed, and for which he was ideally suited: being the first and only "rural reporter" of the local radio station in Dinh Tuong province. The outcome of the war in the Delta was going to be determined by the peasantry. For both the Government and the Viet Cong, the peasants seemed little more than pawns. Rural hamlets might typically be "controlled" by the Government during the day, but by the Viet Cong/National Liberation Front at night. To be a peasant in the Delta meant seeing your children conscripted by one side or the other. It meant either abandoning homestead and paddy for the only-somewhat-greater security of ramshackle settlements on the outskirts of towns, or remaining in the countryside, always careful to give neither side reason to suspect sympathy with the "enemy."

What Mr. Cam was doing with his portable tape recorder would have been familiar to any reporter covering the farm beat in the American Midwest: speaking with farmers about the weather, the crops, livestock, fertilizers, health questions and the markets. But he was also doing much more: giving voice to the voiceless, telling the local "powers" what their too-routinely neglected fellow citizens were thinking; building bridges where all too few existed before.

So why will I never forget the two-paragraph letter from Mr. Cam that was delivered to me that morning?

Because after a first paragraph, thanking me profusely for having made it possible for him to have been doing what he had been doing ...

The next paragraph, in the same clear handwriting, said that "I want to inform you" that he would be dead by the time I received his letter.

But why???????? We had been together only a couple of days previously. He had been in seemingly robust health. Enemies? But who??? Killed? But why? And what sort of death could I imagine which would have included the time to write, apparently quite calmly, such a letter, in English, with someone's promise that it would be delivered to me? My questions to the Province Chief, the area military commander, Vietnamese Information Service counterparts and Mr. Cam's family all seemed simply to slip into the ether. If any of them knew, it was clearly to be kept from me. Had any of them been involved? I couldn't help but wonder, but I would never know.

I paid for, and Ms Tri organized, the type of funeral procession through the town accorded the passing of especially esteemed citizens, with mourners both genuine and paid, drummers, monks and Buddhist flags. There was no body. I never learned more than that which Mr. Cam himself had told me in his last letter.

Although I have not — yet — found Mr. Cam's letter, I have found a carbon copy of the one which I wrote later that day to his parents. Some of it reads as follows:

"Mr. Cam was one of my closest friends in Vietnam. I had complete respect and admiration for him. I know of no one in Vietnam who was more patriotic and dedicated than he. He not only made me have great respect for the Vietnamese people, but his actions and his spirit made me feel humble and grateful that I could be fortunate enough to have the opportunity to work in Vietnam to assist in building the type of nation that Mr. Cam desired ....

"Mr. Cam loved his rural reporter work and performed it excellently. He could have chosen a much easier job instead, and he could have chosen a job which would have paid more money. But Mr. Cam was never interested in easy work, nor in money. He was interested only in helping the Vietnamese people as best he could .... His background and his dedication made him the perfect man for this work. Because of his personality and his love of people, he was widely-known and respected by many different types of people in Ding Tuong, including peasants, soldiers, cadre, officials, teachers, students, laborers and American advisors.

"Mr. Cam felt in his heart all of the tragedies of Vietnam, but his heart was also full of pride because he was Vietnamese. He once told me that when he was younger he occasionally felt unhappy because he had not been born in a richer, happier country. But he had learned, he said, to realize that he was extremely fortunate to have been born in

Vietnam and to have lived at this time, when he could fight and work to help his people become free, happy and prosperous .....

"I will always be proud to have known Mr. Cam and to have had him as a close friend. Mr. Cam sometimes said that he and I were 'brothers in spirit.' I feel today as though my brother had died.

"Please accept .... please be assured ...."

I've thought of Tran-Doan-Cam as my second "K.I.A." — a second individual who, like University of Helsinki Rektor Magnifikus Linkomies died when they did because of something that I had gotten them involved in. There may have been others of whom I was unaware.

Although I will never know what actually caused Mr. Cam's death, it surely was somehow connected with the work which I had encouraged and enabled him to do. But I'm quite certain that it was a choice he would have made again.

Misery

Perhaps it was dengue fever. Perhaps it was malaria. In a week it was gone. But there I was, alone in my My Tho home/office, with hallucinations, fever, vomiting and aches everywhere. I would crawl from my bed to the bathroom (not knowing whether, when there, to accommodate the urgent vomiting or the equally urgent diarrhea), then collapse to the bathroom floor trying to summon the strength to crawl back to the bed. On the worst night, hallucinating, I was convinced that I would cease to breath unless I consciously forced each breath — and that, if I fell asleep, I would thus die. That night I dragged myself, disheveled, to my vehicle, drove three blocks to the compound in which a volunteer U.S. civilian doctor was staying, and pounded on his door. He gave me some pills. I went home, slept, and presumably continued to inhale and exhale nevertheless.

But when it became known in the community that I was ill, I began to get visitors calling to express their condolences: bearded elders, teachers, counterpart officials, military officers.

Lying in bed, drenched with sweat and absolutely inert, I would hear the soft knocking on the front door. I would struggle up, put on my bathrobe, go to the door and open it. Exchanging a mishmash of

English, Vietnamese and French phrases, we would bow solemnly to one another as I invited them to sit.

Tea now needed to be served, so I shuffled groggily to the kitchen to put the water on. Back to the living/dining room; they expressing their condolences, I thanking them. Then back to the kitchen for the tea and cups, then awkward conversation and then, finally, after more bowing and taking of hands, and they would leave. I would sink to the floor, and eventually crawl back into bed ..until the next knocking on the door. These visits were, I knew, genuine expressions of esteem. But this was a cultural tradition which presumed, I was sure, that the ill person had one or more caretakers. If only ...

When I was about to leave My Tho for Oslo, I was presented with a piece of parchment and a medal, as were most departing American advisors. I was told, though, that my citation (it was some sort of Order of the Mighty Lion or some such) was, in fact, rather unusual, and actually did reflect some esteem. Whether true or not, it was nice to hear.

Making Trouble

Although it was of course denied then, everyone accepts now — including the late Robert McNamara — that there was commanding and constant pressure on all of Uncle Sam's people in South Vietnam to "report" what was positive; to see the conflict as Washington (in its distance and ignorance) perceived it. This folly was compounded by the fact that most of us were "in country" only 12 months or so: as someone famously observed, we "did not have a dozen years of experience in Vietnam ... but one year of experience twelve times."

Many can give instances of this, all the way from the '50s, when we first were denying that it was a civil war, to the final agonies and tragedies of the fall of Saigon's forces, and America's aims, in 1974 — when Ambassador Graham Martin, refusing to admit the obvious, forbade official Americans everywhere to prepare for evacuation (and in doing so, to protect and rescue the thousands of Vietnamese who, having trusted and worked closely with us, were to be sacrificed when we finally, in panic and in spite of Ambassador Martin, fled.)

My part of the war was tiny, tiny. But because I wasn't happy being there, because I was with one of the smallest organizations, because I learned much from Rand Corporation friends and from Vietnamese interlocutors ...and because, I suppose, of a certain ornery streak and probably a disinclination to be an unquestioning team player, I at least contributed a tiny bit to the small flow of somewhat more "honest" verbiage which was, however, at each higher level of command, shaped, squelched, denied, ignored and "corrected."

I was, for some 18 months in 1965-67, the representative of JUSPAO, the "Joint United States Public Affairs Office," in two very different provinces southwest of Saigon, in the Vietnamese Delta. In each, we had an American "province team," modeled after the "country team" which, in every Embassy, brings together the various sections and bureaucratic entities in the building. The Embassy country teams, though, have a powerful chairman: the Ambassador. Our province teams had no such head-knocker — unless, as was unlikely, the several civilians would concede this role to our American military member.

In Kien Tuong province, a poor and Godforsaken spot in the Plain of Reeds, our province team comprised the Major who commanded the Special Forces teams, the chief of the local USAID office, the CIA representative ... and me. Each month a report had to be put together, following a format set by the military. And each month we rotated the responsibility for its drafting.

The format had about eight questions. For each, there was hardly space for more than 200 words or so. The eighth asked: "Do you have any problems? Identify."

The first month that I was to draft the team's answer I skipped over this, as had my colleagues each time. But when my turn came the next time, I wasn't willing to let this one go.

"Yes," I wrote, adding something like this:

"The indigenous population of this province are ethnic Vietnamese, Buddhist, poor farmers, and at least passive supporters of the Viet Cong. Our mission is complicated by the fact that our side is, at present, made up almost entirely of outsiders: Catholic refugees from North Vietnam (including the province chief and local forces commander), Chinese and Cambodian special forces units, and Americans. This is the basic problem, and challenge."

My USAID colleague applauded this. The CIA rep went along with it reluctantly ..."But this will never get through," he said. The Special Forces major said it was stupid ...and that this wasn't the meaning of the question. But he was outvoted by the civilians, 3-1, so the report "went forward."

There were corresponding multi-agency "teams" at the Corps level, and in Saigon. But en route from the province to Corps it had to pass through the MAC/V (military advisory command, Vietnam) Division headquarters, headed by a tall, ramrod straight colonel. The Division headquarters was just outside of My Tho, the capital of my other province, Dinh Tuong, where I spent most of each week. He called me in and was, as he would say, "f—-ing furious."

"What is this bullshit, Dickerman?" he shouted, although I was just on the other side of his desk.

"Well, (whatever his first name was), it asked whether we had any problems, and we identified the main one," I said — in this conversation, as in every other with an American military officer in Vietnam, assiduously avoiding the word "Sir" least I be conceding some degree of command authority to him.

"This is goddamned not what this question is about, Dickerman," he yelled again.

"It asked us to identify the problem."

"A PROBLEM, Dickerman, is that you don't have enough mortar rounds so you can't conduct H&I fire, Or you don't have a needed something or other.

"And the most important thing, Dickerman, is that anyone who is stupid enough to name a problem in a report like this had Goddamned better say right then what action he has taken to solve this problem. That may not be true in civilian life. But in the Army, if we have problems, we Goddamned well solve them."

He ordered me to delete my (our!) response. I declined.

He said he would finish my Goddamned career; he would throw me out of the country. I left.

Some days later my office in Saigon said that I was being put in for a "meritorious honor award."

"Evidently," my boss' boss explained while shouting into the field telephone, "you pissed off the military. A general wants your ass out of there. So you must be doing something right.

"Congratulations."

There are many routes to glory.

What B-52s "Don't Do" But Did

"WHAM" — "Win Hearts & Minds" — was the militarese for what we "psychwarriors" were supposedly doing in South Vietnam. One of the tools of our trade was the leaflet — rectangular pieces of paper, perhaps 3 x 5 inches in size, which were dropped by the millions by our committed psyops aircraft. The messages might "invite" people to come over to the Government's side, or they might threaten nasty things if they continued their warfare.

I was awakened one night by a long rumble of apparently huge explosions, some distance away. I learned the explanation at the military's briefing the next morning. A Viet Cong unit had been seen the day before moving northwest of town. The U.S. advisors had called in a strike by B-52s based in Guam, 2,600 miles away.

"That must have scared any who survived," I said. "We'll do a psyops leaflet drop warning them that there will be more to come."

"No you won't," said the MAC/V lieutenant colonel.

"And why not???"

"Because you don't use B-52 strikes against tactical targets," said the colonel. "It's like trying to kill gnats with a sledge hammer. And a really, really expensive one."

"But I thought that's what you just told me you did?" said I.

"Right," he said, ending the conversation. And such tactical B-52 strikes continued 'til we left Vietnam. (An individual B-52F, according to the Air University Review website, could "deliver" one hundred and eight 500-pound bombs, dropping them from 30,000 feet, the bombs landing before anyone on the ground even heard the planes. And the planes flew not individually, but in formations. "In the 18 months from June 1965 through December 1966, SAC B-52s in Southeast Asia dropped more than 130,000 tons of high explosives on nearly 800 missions." That was more than the total tonnage of bombs dropped in Europe in World War II.)

Oh: did I say that the "gnats" won the war?

On the Mekong

There was also a sledgehammer vs gnat problem on the Mekong River, upriver from where I was living, in My Tho. As elsewhere in the Delta it was difficult even for our Vietnamese allies to tell which settlements might be "friendly" or "VC," and, in fact, what any individual might be.

The Navy started deploying the River Patrol Boats of its "Brown Water Navy" in the Mekong during my 1965-67 tour. I don't recall meeting any of them, but was often told by David Elliott, the Vietnamese-speaking Rand Corporation analyst who spent much of his time interviewing Viet Cong prisoners and defectors of one of the problems that was occurring:

"The Navy's boats carry maps which purport to show which hamlets are 'friendly' and which aren't. But partly because all is in such flux, they aren't always accurate. In any case, if a Navy boat is fired upon from any settlement, they respond, sometimes also calling in air support. What seems to sometimes happen is that the VC, who might not be able to take out a hamlet by themselves, sneak near the hamlet and fire on a passing Navy boat. In three or four cases that I know of, we Americans have then, within minutes, wiped out the village ourselves."

"Free Fire Zones"

But our biggest problem of this nature — for those of us actually working on the ground, and with actual Vietnamese human beings (!) — were the bombs dropped indiscriminately in areas of the Delta which pilots, returning to their carriers off shore, were told were "free fire zones." The planes couldn't return to their carriers with ordnance on board, so, just as some Huey gunners considered any water buffalo to be a "VC water buffalo," these aircraft crews were given to understand that anything in such identified areas was "enemy."

The worst instance with which I became personally involved occurred in "my" province of Kien Tuong. A group of "friendly" villagers in several sampans had been following a canal to a regional market, accompanied by their district chief, a Vietnamese Army officer. They had cleared the trip with their local Vietnamese authorities. A plane, presumably from a carrier off shore, attacked them, killing almost all.

My respect for our American troops was greatest for those working, like me, with actual Vietnamese in hamlets, villages and towns; much less for those living in Saigon and on large in-country bases, who had little contact with Vietnamese other than the ubiquitous "bar girls"; and least of all for the aircraft crews who never even set foot in the country, but flew off of carriers and from Guam to kill people they knew absolutely nothing about.

Eliminating the Problem

There was a term in the first world war for the not uncommon shooting of lieutenants in the back as they were leading charges. In war situations, it's not difficult to extinguish folks who may be causing you problems.

In the Vietnamese Delta at the time I was there virtually all of us Americans, whether military or civilian, were "advisors" to Vietnamese advisees. It was supposed to be a symbiotic relationship — but in that situation of stress, danger, and inter-cultural and inter-institutional conflict, these relationships could literally mean life or death. In my work, if I couldn't affect the performance of an advisee through my own persuasion, example, or (yes, financial enticement), then I could complain to my higher headquarters, asking them to put pressure on their own advisees/counterparts, so that "my" advisee would be ordered through his own hierarchy to do what I (for better or worse) believed necessary.

My principal problem in this regard was the chief of the Vietnamese Information Service in the Godforsaken province of Kien Tuong, on the Cambodian border in the desolate Plain of Reeds. Mr. Troung had probably been exiled there for some sin, and he couldn't have been, and wasn't, happy that I was making his life even more unpleasant.

Mr. Troung, whom I had been criticizing for not going out to the (admittedly hostile) peasantry enough, then invited me to go with him on such a trip. We would take sampans through various narrow waterways .... a trip from which, I was quite certain, I would never return alive. I feigned reasons to decline the honor.

About that same time, a gruff 2nd lieutenant in the heavily-sandbagged Special Forces B Team at which I bunked on my weekly visits to Moc Hoa confided that he had had just enough "crap" from his Vietnamese 2d Lieutenant counterpart/advisee. I clearly understood that he intended to kill this man at the first (deniable) opportunity.

A week later this American lieutenant was dead; shot by someone when on a patrol. Although it was flimsily deniable, it seemed clear that the advisee had eliminated his advisor before the advisor could eliminate him. (Yes: the names of such casualties are also inscribed on the melancholy wall of the Vietnam War Memorial on the National Mall.)

The VC's Atrocities

Of course the Viet Cong/National Liberation Front were also practicing indiscriminate killing. Their firepower was much less than ours. But ethically, is it arguable any different to kill face-to-face, "in cold blood," than from a B-52 at 30,000 feet?

The two worst VC atrocities in area, during my watch, were:

The slaughter of some 45 peasants — men, women and children — as they lay sleeping in a pagoda in the village of Tan An, on the road between My Tho and Saigon. The crime of these poorest of the poor? They were, with picks and shovels, digging an irrigation canal paid for by the Government.

And a rickety bus, full of women and children, which was mined as it made its way along a dangerous road, through the Plain of Reeds, between my two provinces. I believe that some 30 were killed. There were also a handful of survivors, given triage by a Special Forces (enlisted) medic who, with his colleagues, came to the scene as quickly as they could.

Basically, it was risky — life threatening — for any Vietnamese in a rural area to become identified with either side. I sometimes wondered what the long term genetic consequence would be of the elimination from the gene pool of so many who showed leadership ability. We had our assassination lists. So did they.

Targeted Killing

The Viet Cong road blocks at which the labor leader Mr. Tuc admitted having been stopped, and thus forced to pay a "tax," were a fact of life (and/or death) for anyone venturing out on the roadways at night, or even during the day on some roads. One could never know where they might be, or when; just as one couldn't know whether a road was mined or not.

There was said to be (I never met them and can't confirm it) one "program" which very efficiently targeted, and killed, Viet Cong activists who clearly were not "just civilians." Supposedly there was, in the Delta, a rickety bus which traveled the riskier roads at dusk. When the bus was stopped at a VC check point (and toll station), its passengers — supposedly a motley crew of "bad guys" from the gangs of Harlem, opened fire. The bus would then drive off.

What I then wondered, and still wonder today, is: when these guys got home did they get other Government jobs? Are they today retired, on federal pensions?????? And how had they been recruited in the first place???

Over-ruled, Over-run

Of more consequence was the failure of those who knew better to thwart the committing of an American combat division to the densely-populated Vietnamese Delta,

Since the earliest stages of American involvement in Vietnam, in the mid-50's, the response to each escalating difficulty was to escalate the number of American troops .... "advisors" first, and then troops. But things rarely improved; South Vietnamese society failed to coalesce around the Governments and leaderships which we chose for them; resistance, both indigenous and fueled from the North, continued. More American fighting power ...more American personnel ...more money ...more facilities, more air power, more defoliation, more "hearts and minds," more PsyOps ... "more" was always the answer.

One-third of South Vietnam's population lived southwest of Saigon, in the fertile, very densely-populated Mekong Delta. Here, unlike north of Saigon, the conflict clearly was a civil war: neighbor against neighbor; South Vietnamese against South Vietnamese (and their American allies). No North Vietnamese units operated in the Delta. One could argue, as some did, whether the "National Liberation Front for the Liberation of South Vietnam" — which we called "Viet Cong" — was a tool of the North Vietnamese party and regime, or not. But all of the evidence from Rand Corporation interviews with prisoners and defectors, and other intelligence, indicated that it was local people, rural people, who were so successfully hamstringing South Vietnamese travel, commerce and development; who controlled at night what we claimed to control by daylight.

When we — we being virtually all "advisors" in the Delta, both military and civilian — learned that Washington and Saigon were planning to put an American combat division into the Delta, I knew of no American colleague who thought it anything other than an absolutely inane idea. In the heavily populated Delta, even the Vietnamese had difficulty knowing who was "friendly," who was "VC" and who was in between. How in the world would Americans be able to do so?

And how could American combat troops, with their heavy equipment and their extraordinary fire power, be anything other than "the elephant in the chicken coop"? Much of the Delta was a mesh of canals and rice patties: American tanks and armored personnel carriers could not help but smash these on every operation. And like the U.S. Navy "riverine patrols" on the Mekong, there was every likelihood that, if fired upon, the Americans would respond with devastating firepower, destroying everything ... including what would, inevitably, sometimes turn out to have been "friendlies."

Unanimously, we told Saigon — we told the Embassy, we told MAC/V, we told our various superiors — that this was an idea which should absolutely be stopped; a decision which could only go wrong.

Not that anyone had asked our views, of course. And our military colleagues were set straight immediately: their job was not to object ...their job was to carry out the mission. Yes Sir!!! They were silenced. And they set to work laying the groundwork for the huge new base just west of My Tho.

That left, still objecting, the meek civilian voices of the USAID rep, the CIA station, my own one-man JUSPAO office ... and the American who knew more about the Vietnamese society and the war in the Delta than any number of his compatriots combined, David Elliott of the Rand Corporation.

But of course it all fell on deaf ears. The U.S. 9th Infantry Division arrived in mid-1969 ...the first all-draftee division to be committed to Vietnam. Everything that we had worried about ensued. And more.

When the draw-down of American troops in Vietnam finally got serious, in 1972, this U.S. Ninth Infantry Division was among the very first to go. One can only imagine the cost, in lives, dikes, rice fields, families, matériel and honor, that must be charged to an absolutely inexcusable, unjustifiable decision. As a bumper sticker years later was to read: "Ignorance and Arrogance Make Bad Foreign Policy."

And "yes sir!" can be the worst answer of all.

My Escape

A small lie for a good cause.

Yes, it was a bit of a lie ... but it could have been true. It was, let us say, plausible. And if, as the cynics claimed, "a diplomat is one who is paid to lie for his country," then why not employ just a little bit of this diplomatic skill for one's own desperate need?

Especially after two lonely years in Somalia! And a year and a half, both lonely and dangerous, in the Vietnamese Delta! All because of unspeakable awfulness of the personnel department: a warren filled, I knew, with married men ("Otherwise, I'd love to go myself"), with fathers ("Unfortunately, because of them, I just can't"): gnomes ready to sacrifice every Foreign Service bachelor to defeat the nasty 'Cong.

But somehow my luck had changed: God had come to my aid. I had received a letter that my bid for the press attaché job in Norway had been accepted .... and I was to report to the Embassy in Oslo two months hence.

AMEN!!!!!!!!!!!!!!!!!!!!!!

But my Big Boss, Barry Zorthian, an Armenian-American legend who was to be involved in every single disastrous decision made for years by the Saigon Embassy's "country team," would have none of it.

"Oslo!???" he nearly shouted at me when I went to Saigon to show him the precious letter: my ticket to safety and freedom ... and women.

"Ridiculous! A war going on here .... a desperate need for officers ... and they are going to pull you out to go to OSLO??!!! I will stop this right now," and he reached for the phone.

"But Barry, Barry ..." I pleaded.

"But Barry ... wait, wait ... you know ..." (thinking as fast and and desperately as I could) " ... it's the Norwegians who give the Nobel Peace Prize."

"Grunt," he muttered, awaiting the operator.

"And the Norwegians are really against what we're doing here. They really are."

"Well so are a lot of people," he muttered.

"And there is NO one in the Embassy in Oslo who has been here in Vietnam, who can explain what's really going on."

"Well, bully, Dickerman; we need you here more. No shit."

"But Barry, what a lot of people are worried about is that Norway may give the Nobel Peace Prize to Ho-chi-Minh!"

"wHAT????????"

"That's right, Barry: the Nobel Peace Prize to Ho-chi-Minh. That would cause some problems, wouldn't it!?," I said.

"Well shit," said Barry. "Wouldn't that be the Goddamnedest ...."

He put down the phone.

So I was going to Oslo. It was going to be tough, but someone would have to do it ....

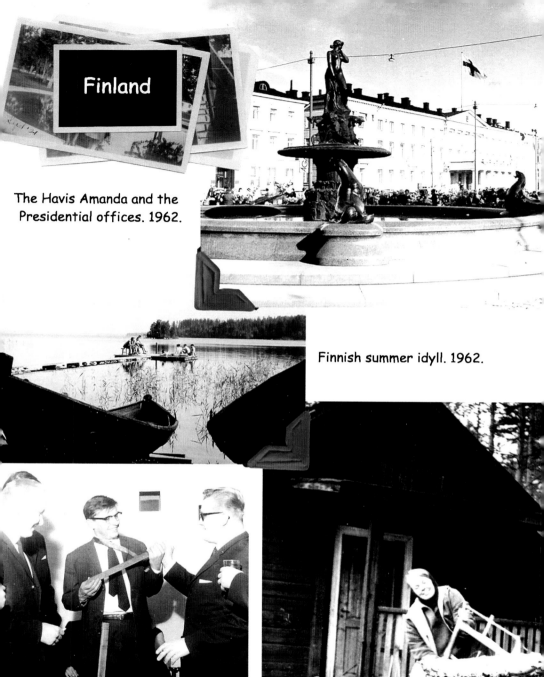

Finland

The Havis Amanda and the Presidential offices. 1962.

Finnish summer idyll. 1962.

Being made an Honorary Member of the Finnish National Student Union. 1963.

Vickan at the sawhorse. 1963.

Students who later were beaten when they tried to parad protesting nuclear testing in the Wes OR East. 1962.

With Vickan and, apparently, beer. 1963.

Gloria Steinem in the 1960's (from Wikipedia).

Somalia

CRD and USIS colleague Hussein Mussa at the entranceway to the USIS American Library and offices Catercorner, but not visible here, was our Embassy. In the foreground CRD's "corps diplomatique" motorscooter. 1964.

The oldest quarter of Mogadishu, probably now destroyed. The white octagonal tower was the Finance Miniistry. The pink building housed other government offices. 1964.

A political rally on the Mogadishu waterfront. 1964.

B U L L E T I N

USIS LIBRARY

HAPPY NEW YEAR FROM THE USIS LIBRARY!

A fun moment in our USIS Mogadishu library. 1965.

JANUARY 1965

CORSO PRIMO LUGLIO
M OGADISCIO

3   · No.

The "acting director" of our USIS/USAID English Language School with the new graduating class. 1965

Young Somali men with their sticks, knives and a spear. So common was the gesture of the gent who is the third from the left that we called it "the Somali salute." 1965.

With young friends in the highlands of northern Somalia. 1963.

Somali men warming up for the annual "stick fight" in Afgoi. The new crops were believed to need shedded blood to grow. The government urged that sticks be substituted for spears. 1965.

South Vietnam

The author, probably scared to death, trying not to show it as he accompanies a musical troupe (sic!) along a Delta waterway. 1966.

Getting around in downtown Moc Hoa during flooding of the entire Plain of Reeds. 1966.

Passing out goodies to peasants in the
severely flooded Plain of Reeds. 1966.

Orphans made happier because of students
inspired by Huynh-thi=Tri. 1967.

Ms Huynh-thi-Tri.
1967.

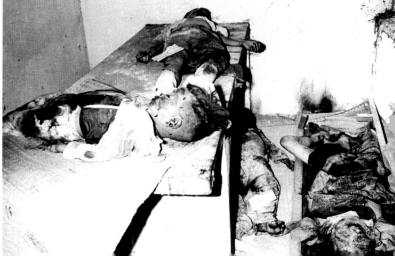

Peasant children killed
by Viet Cong as they
ept with their families
in a pagoda in Tan An.
1966.

Norway

On the Palace lawn on Norway's National Day. May 17, 1968.

CRD's Oslo home on a spring day. 1969.

A summer picnic in the Nordmarka woods bordering Oslo. 1967.

On a hike in beautiful Fjærlandsfjord. 1968.

Margrethe her national dress. 1968.

Dad and stepmother Brookie above the Geiranger fjord. 1969.

Author skiing. 1968.

Apollo 11 Astronauts cheered along Oslo's Drottningsgata. 1969.

Escorting Neil Armstrong into the Norwegian Parliament. 1969.

Midsummer bonfire on Vega. 1969.

Iceland

Icelandic ponies
along the South
Coast. 1973.

Reykjavik from
a distance. 1973.

With Christina
and Rati along-
side an Icelanic
glacier. 1974.

Crazy sister Anne
at the Icelandic
"beach." 1974.

Icelandic vistas. 1974.

Midwinter noontime from home. 1974.

Midsummer camping. 1974.

Joe Glazer sings one more time for Icelanders Bryndís and Jón Baldwin.

Barbados/ Caribbean

Seven day workweeks, but a great plac to live. Barbados 1983-85.

CRD presenting a 1,300 volume "American Library" to Grenada's University Center. The couple to the left are Governor General Sir Paul Scoon and Lady Scoon. February 1985.

Barbados 1983-85.

Sisterly love.
Julia to the left;
Anneke to the right.
Barbados, 1985.

Parents, daughters
& doll. Barbados 1983.

Trinidad & Tobago

Ambassador Sheldon J. Krys (center on stairs) with the staff of the American Embassy in Port of Spain. 198

CRD with the Boss: Ambassador Sheldon J. Krys. 1988.

Sunday Guardian MAGAZINE   July

Chargé (!) Dickerman with T&T President Noor Hassanali and Mrs. Hassanali. 1988.

Anneke & Julia with playmates. Port-of-Spain 1986.

Denmark

Roskilde Cathedral. 1958.

Thatched roof home near
Roskilde. 1958.

My first Danish "parents" being visited
by Elsabet's parents. 1957-58.

Elisa. 1957-58.

Embassy families at our home in Hellerup, Denmark. 1991.

"Wrong hat, Mr Dickerman???" The Queen's Lord Chamberlain inspects my attire.

Ib Koch-Olsen leading a class at the folk high school. 1958.

Julia and Anneke: grown up beautiful. 2009.

Julia (left), Anneke, and Daddy post-Cold War. 1992.

Norway, 1967-70

Getting There

Euphoric, I packed my few things in My Tho and tidied up my office "chron file" — which basically was piles of papers starting in one corner, marching along the wall to the next, then to the third. "Where are the files?" asked my successor, Don Mathes. "Right there," I said, pointing to the files. He destroyed them.

My predecessor had been responsible for four provinces. I inherited only two of them: Dinh Tuong and Kien Tuong. They were again divided when I left: Don inherited Dinh Tuong; someone else would work desolate Kien Tuong alone. And thus it was that we assigned more and more Americans, both military and civilian, without it doing a bit of good.

But Vietnam's problems were the last thing on my mind as my plane finally took off from Saigon's airport. Never, except when departing Somalia, have I ever felt so very relieved. To Oslo!

I stopped in Bangkok, Bombay, Katmandu, New Dehli, Agra, Beirut and Istanbul en route to my dreamland, my Valhalla. Walking along a tree-shaded boulevard in Istanbul, I was astonished when a lovely blonde, coming the opposite direction, said "Bob! Hej Bob!" It was so unlikely that she eventually had to tell me just who she was: Bambi Gahmberg, a sweetheart I'd dated in Helsinki six years previously, now married to a Turkish gent. It was a good omen.

Norway!!!!

Norway!!! When I'd chosen the Foreign Service over the city desk of The *Chicago Tribune*, I'd naively imagined that I'd be spending my entire career in postings to the paradises of Denmark, Finland, Sweden, Norway and Iceland. The tours in Somalia and South Vietnam had disabused me of those illusions. But now I'd be back, and in what it seemed to me was the most desirable job in any Embassy: that of press attaché. And with my still-recalled Danish, augmented by some use of "Finlands Svenska" in Helsinki, I could expect to speak Norwegian reasonably well before too long.

Having assured Barry Zorthian that I'd do all that I could to dissuade the Norwegians from awarding the Nobel Peace Prize to Ho-chi-Minh, and having, to my considerable relief, reached my 30th birthday without being killed, I packed my stuff, introduced my successor, bade farewell to my local interlocutors, and left. Norway, I was sure, would be splendid.

Pre-Oil Norway

The Norway in which I worked from 1967-70 was not the Norway you would visit today:

At an Embassy "country team" meeting in 1969, Harold Flaata, the last remaining officer from a once-large Marshall Plan staff, held up a corked laboratory beaker containing a thick black liquid. It would soon be announced, he said, that the Phillips corporation had found formations off the coast of Stavanger containing "very significant" volumes of oil and gas.

"This," Harold said, "will change almost everything."

And it did.

The CIA World Fact Book estimates Norway's per capita income in 2010, at PPP (purchasing power parity) to have been $59,100. This contrasts with $47,400 for the U.S. , $39,000 for Sweden, $35,100 for the United Kingdom, and $34,200 for Japan. In the decades since 1970, Norway has become the world's fifth largest exporter of oil, one of the world's largest holder of reserve currencies ..."Europe's

Kuwait," and a land of "blue eyed Arabs."

But in the late '60s, Norway was still the poor country cousin to neighboring Sweden. Virtually everyone in Oslo had close ties to family along the coast, in the valleys, in the fjords, or in the mountains. Norway is still gorgeous, its egalitarian democratic and economic values still enviable, and its people still wonderfully balanced blends of physical, intellectual and spiritual strengths. But as in Bavaria, the bucolic seems now to be more of a cherished folk tradition than an everyday reality.

In any case, Norway seemed to me to be almost perfect. (It still does, in fact.) But what was not perfect in the late Sixties, of course, was the way in which the United States was perceived abroad. The respect and gratitude which we had earned in World War II, through the subsequent Marshall Plan, and as "Leader of the Free World" could not continue forever, of course. But the tarnishing of America's image was hastened by President Kennedy's assassination on November 23, 1963, by President Johnson's much clumsier rhetoric in articulating America's actions, and by increasing awareness abroad of American poverty and racism.

Through the Sixties, there was ever-increasing opposition to the Vietnam war. "We," with our "culture of violence," had killed President Kennedy and Medgar Evens in 1963, Malcolm X in 1965, and then, in 1968, Martin Luther King, Jr., on April 4th, followed by Robert F. Kennedy two months later. Large areas of Washington DC, Detroit, Newark, Chicago, Pittsburgh, Louisville, New York, and other cities were set aflame following Dr. King's killing. A year later we learned of the massacre by American soldiers, following sexual abuse and torture, of as many as 500 unarmed peasants in the Vietnamese village of My Lai. In May 1970 Kent State University students protesting the Vietnam war were fired upon by the Ohio National Guard, killing four, wounding nine, and causing further national and international alarm. In Stockholm, Prime Minister Olaf Palme joined demonstrators marching to the American Embassy. Black Panthers leader Bobby Seale drew a huge crowd at the University of Oslo (with me sliding deeper into my seat when he asked "Who here is from the American Embassy?????") And Norwegian Broadcasting's new correspondent in Washington, Ole Christian Lagesen, never missed an opportunity to tell his listeners and viewers that "the American Dream is dead." Rightly concerned lest such views totally obscure what Scandinavians could still admire about the United States, many centrists and conservatives drew attention to "The Other America": that of Senator Fulbright (conveniently forgetting his long support for segregation), similarly anti-war Senator Eugene McCarthy, Justice Thurgood Marshall, and others.

The murder of Dr. King was especially shocking to Norwegians. With a large delegation of fellow Atlantans, Dr. King had come to Oslo only three years earlier to accept the 1964 Nobel Peace Prize. Now the Laureate then honored as "the first person in the Western world to have shown us that a struggle can be waged without violence," was himself, at age 39, shot dead. Most Norwegians heard the news, as did I, at breakfast on Friday, April 5th.

Through the 1,100 mile length of Norway, flags at homes and offices were raised (or lowered) to half-mast. Norwegian cameramen and photographers grouped outside our Embassy on Drottningsgata to show our own lowered flag. But it seemed that the only flag in all of Oslo which was not lowered was ours.

Press Attaché Dickerman, increasingly agitated, was in and out of the office of Ambassador Margaret Joy Tibbetts.

"Madame Ambassador, we must lower that flag!!!!!!" I was saying.

"I understand, Bob. But only the President can order the flag lowered."

"But you're the President's representative here, Madame Ambassador, and we must lower it."

With some trepidation, she so ordered. And within an hour or so, President Johnson did as well. It was, we understood, the first time in American history that the flag had been ordered lowered for a "private" citizen.

Nights and Daze

But it was a beautiful spring in 1967. A beautiful city, a beautiful country, a great and even prestigious job for a 30-year-old bachelor ... and this after several years of loneliness and self-pity in Somalia and South Vietnam. It was the 60's: long hours in a job I loved, but also the girls, the outdoors, the sailing, skiing, drinking and partying.

On weekdays I awoke at 6, showered, and had listened to the news on Norwegian Radio, the BBC and the Voice of America before arriving at the Embassy at 7:30. There were then seven (!) daily newspapers in Oslo alone. My information assistant, Leif Sommerseth, and I divided them up and put together the Embassy's internal press briefing. We then selected texts from Washington for the "USIS News Bulletin," mailed daily to media throughout the country. Other tasks, including sending Norwegian "comment" back to Washington, filled the afternoons. From Monday through Thursday, there were often obligatory social/representational events. Because I was the lone Norwegian-speaking bachelor in an Embassy headed by a single woman, I very often found myself, in tuxedo, at the "low end" of the Ambassador's dinner table, balancing the gender scales and making awkward conversation. On weekends, blessedly, there were no such events. Norwegians, quite sensibly, much preferred to spend that part of the week at their cabins in the mountains, or on their boats in the fjords.

Wolf!!!!!

Sometimes the dual roles of cultural diplomat and propagandist did not mix well. At one point we brought to Oslo Lukas Foss, the famously avant-garde composer and musical director of the Buffalo Philharmonic Orcestra, to conduct a concert for the Norwegian "New Music" organization.

The concert went well (but who was I to judge?) and afterwards, because USIS had made Foss' visit possible, I was invited to an after-the-event party in a large apartment not far from the center of town. The leading lights of Oslo's musical and artistic avant garde were there, as were a wonderful number of most attractive young women. Several were fawning over Foss, but several others were grouped together on a carpet. The liquor flowed. And I invited myself to sit with these latter lovelies. At first it was going well: "Are you here with Lukas?" purred one, seeming to indicate that an affirmative answer to that might find me with her the next morning.

I sensed the danger, and avoided it as long as I could. But finally it came out: I worked at the American Embassy.

"ULF!!!! A WOLF!" screamed my questioner, alarming the others as well. "He's one of them! American Embassy! American Embassy!"

"Wolf! How did he get in here?? American Embassy! Out!! Out!!! Out!!!!," said others, scurrying away.

Foss watched this dreamily, dark eyes half-closed, nearly smothered in a deep sofa, entwined with any number of sweet and cooing admirers. He was certainly not going to help me, compatriot or not. And very soon ...very, very soon, I was out on the street, and headed home. Alone and resentful.

"Damn Lyndon Johnson!," I muttered.

"LBJ! LBJ! How much else did you screw up today?"

I'm So Sorry, Liv

The two most obscure and inconsequential "periodicals" for which I was responsible were, surely, "The USIS Library Bulletin"s in Somalia and Norway. These noted the new books in our library collections, and might carry an article on a speaker we would be having, or a speaker or performer whom we had hosted recently.

The "USIS Oslo Library Bulletin" was printed in-house and mailed, as I recall, to two or three hundred library members.

My boss, Bill Astill, was one of those people who collected photographs of notables whom they had met, ideally pictured together with them; but in any case with an autograph ("To My Good Friend William ....")

One day Bill announced to me that he had met a young Norwegian actress whom he was certain would have a great future. He had asked her if we might feature her in the "USIS Oslo Library Bulletin," and she had agreed. She had, in fact, offered to come to the Embassy that very afternoon to be photographed for the article. Would I please see that this was done?

But I claimed to have something else to do ... probably involving imbibing and flirting in one of the nearby outdoor cafés. So I left the photographing job to a Norwegian colleague.

The young actress was Liv Ullman, then 29; two years younger than I.

Might she even have gone out for a drink with me???? Might we have fallen head over heels in love? Might she today be Liv Ullman Dickerman??????? Or I Bob Dickerman Ullman???? Might it have made absolutely no difference whatsoever?

Of such concerns is misery made.

Far from Home

Like all diplomatic cars in Norway, my black Volvo had, in addition to a Norwegian license plate, an oval plate saying "CD" ...Corps Diplomatique (although the Norwegians joked, not without reason, that it meant "Chauffeur Drunken").

At a gasoline station in Northern Norway one summer, the attendant noticed the unusual plate and asked me what country "CD" was.

"Costa del Sol," I said.

"Oh," he said. "I've heard of your country."

James Bond Dickerman

It's inevitable that, if you work in an American Embassy, you're going to be accused of, or at least teased about, being "CIA." Especially frustrating, it seemed to me, was my impression that the more competent one seemed to be, the better one spoke the language, the better informed one was (not that I ever met all of these criteria!), the more apt one was to get this accusation.

And this wasn't just from our "host country" contacts. My own first cousin, a Fort Collins physician and artist, confessed to me some years ago that she had been "so disappointed" when she finally was persuaded that: (1) my dad had not been a chiropractor, but an osteopath, and (2) that I had not been "CIA" but a boring old Foreign Service Officer.

It was an annoyance. As naïve as ever, I would probably have closed down most of our intelligence offices if I could have. But still: if one's contacts were going to endure this suspicion anyway: shouldn't there be some James Bond style "benefits"?

If not the cars, then the girls? Okay, maybe just one????

It happened just once. The "Prague Spring" of 1968 was an exciting one all through Western Europe. The Czechoslovakian people were on the verge of liberating themselves from 20 years of tight Soviet/Communist control. Young Czechs and Slovaks exalted in this new freedom. All through Scandinavia and the Continent fascinating, exuberant kids in their late teens and early twenties were hitchhiking, waving their tri-colored flags.

But on August 21st the idyll ended: Soviet and Warsaw Pact troops invaded Czechoslovakia and ruthlessly brought an end to the reforms, and dreams, of the brief era of "socialism with a human face." Thousands of the students and other young people who were in the West stayed.

My black Volvo had a "CD" sticker on it, identifying me as a diplomat — and thus a lucky fellow who could get his gas tax-free.

When I occasionally filled my tank at the local Esso station, I couldn't help but be flattered by the flirtatious, suggestive remarks of the attractive, English-speaking brunette behind the cash register. Eventually I succumbed, of course, and asked her out.

One thing led to another, as it sometimes does (hmmm: did!). She was from Prague; she had been hitchhiking in Norway when the Soviets invaded; she had remained, and she lived in a dormitory at the University of Oslo.

Many of her Norwegian dormitory mates were, as was common among students at that time, supporters of the "Norway Out of NATO" movement.

"I tell them they are crazy!" she said. "That's why my country has no freedom! I tell them: 'If you get close to succeeding, tell me ... because I'm going to America.'"

But what she most wanted was her infant daughter, whom she'd left behind with her mother when she'd set off for what had been expected to be a single month's wander in Scandinavia. Now she could only very surreptitiously communicate with her mother.

"Can't you help me, darling? Purrrrrrrrrr ....."

And it turned out that I could ...or at least I could try:

Bjørn Sørum, the chief of our audio-visual section at USIS, was also an amateur magician. And he was, in fact, planning to attend an international magicians' congress that spring ... in Prague.

I put the two of them together. And was happy to learn, after Bjørn's return, that he had successfully, and perhaps magically, concealed the infant daughter in his car, and slipped across the border into Austria. Where her mommy was awaiting.

It made a feller feel pretty good. Cloak & Dagger stuff, you know.

A Fast Descent

It was as sudden an evaporating of status as I could imagine.

For the past 36 hours, in January 1969, I'd been Vice President Humphrey's interpretor as he chatted, in Kristiansand, with elderly Norwegian relatives from his mother's side of the family. I'd flown down from Oslo with the Vice President's party in Air Force Two. And, in my press attaché role, I had commandeered, for the Norwegian media, the elegant bar of the town's fanciest hotel. Food? Drinks? Put it on my tab. We'd even, quite unexpectedly, had Mr. Humphrey drop in ... and remain, as he renowned for ... to hold forth with my newsie friends through two late night hours.

But that was yesterday, and last night. The Vice President and his party had left for Washington the next morning, and I took a late-afternoon commercial flight back to Oslo. Pretty exhausted, but still running on the adrenalin a VIP visit like that stimulates, I went from the airport to the Embassy to write and file a story for the Voice of America.

I finished up and, although I hadn't slept for a couple of days, recalled that there was neither milk or bread nor cheese at home. Oslo then had very strict rules limiting almost all retailing to 9 am to 5 pm. It was now about 10:30, so I parked near the train station and went down to the lower level where the single mini-mart in the entire city operated all night long.

I took a small cart and headed down the aisles, finding my milk, bread and cheese. I also put a package of candles in the cart, and some soap and shampoo.

At this time in the evening the shop's customers were mostly pretty grungy gents who, one way or another, had accumulated just enough change to buy yet another beer. I stood behind them in line.

The cashier was perhaps 16. She didn't seem particularly happy in her job, putting up with this particular clientèle.

I placed my milk, cheese, bread, candles, soap and shampoo on the counter. She added them up. I reached for my wallet .. .and had left it at the Embassy. Embarrassed, I tried to explain: "Vice President Humphrey, press attaché, blah blah." And I found, in my pockets, coins enough for perhaps half of the total price.

"Take the candles," I said. "Take the soap! Take the shampoo!"

But she had already removed the milk, bread and cheese.

"Please, Miss!," I said. "I need that food! I haven't eaten since morning."

She looked at me with utter scorn. She'd seen enough guys like me. And there would be more of us, with their lies and excuses, before her quitting time.

She took my change, bagged the candles, soap and the shampoo, and rang them up.

"Next," she said.

Yes, Mr. Ambassador: Yes, Sir

My job as press attaché involved a good many responsibilities. But like every job in an Embassy, the most important was to keep the Ambassador happy. An unhappy Ambassador could make life miserable and, at worst, even get one sent home.

My first Ambassador in Oslo, perhaps the very best for whom I ever worked, was Margaret Joy Tibbetts, one of the very first of the now-common female career American Ambassadors. She had learned enough Norwegian by the time I arrived there that she read the papers herself, and thus called on me only occasionally.

But Ms Tibbetts' successor was a political ambassador of the old school. In fact, he was everything of the old school. And a character.

Phillip Kingsland Crowe had earlier served, under President Eisenhower, as our Ambassador to South Africa and to Ceylon. He loved "Ambassadoring," as he called it, and had gladly accepted this third Presidential call to duty. He was in Oslo from 1968 to 1971, when he was named to Copenhagen because, yes (more of this later), they were actually serving Atlantic salmon in tourist class (he would say with the utmost indignation) on SAS (!).

In any case, when Ambassador Crowe arrived, I became responsible for his morning press briefing. Leif and I would prepare a "daily press briefing" of about three single spaced typed pages. It would include both news and commentary. Copies of this went to each of the Embassy's several sections, where ordinary mortals would simply read it. But His Excellency required that it be read to him.

I sat before his huge desk and read. He rarely interrupted during the political and international news sections, except to characterize various individuals as they were named and, in the case of celebrities and royalty, to ensure that I knew that he or she was " my close friend." The more British they were, and the closer to Prince Philip ("my dear, dear friend"), the more important this was. (He once sent me a courtesy copy of a letter he'd sent to his "dear friend" Henry Luce, the founder and owner of the TIME/LIFE empire, to extend his subscription. He apparently hadn't noticed that this particular "dear friend" had recently died.)

The economic and business news which I delivered elicited more comment. Certain policies were "damned socialist ideas", others were "pure communism." I would also be asked my opinion of "the market": would it go to 1,000?; would it something else? Little did I know: I had no stocks, and couldn't care less.

But the nasty part of each morning's briefing ....the part that more than a few times caused me to fear that I was to be fired immediately ... involved the media commentary: the editorials of the day. "Vietnam" was the primary issue in those years. About half of the Norwegian papers supported us, and about half were opposed. But the support was slipping away; the demonstrations were getting larger and larger, and more and more Norwegian politicians and pundits were giving us "advice."

Ambassador Phillip Kingsland Crowe did not much like this advice:

"Goddamn it, Dickerman. What you're saying is pure Bullshit."

"Sir, this is in today's editorial in Arbeiderbladet, the Labor Party newspaper."

"Pure Goddamned socialism, I say. Well, go ahead ...."

"Well, the commentator on the Norwegian television news last night said ....," and I would paraphrase more condemnation of our doings in Vietnam or elsewhere.

"Goddamnit, Bob, how can you come in here every morning and talk like this??????????"

"Mr. Ambassador, Sir, I ...."

"I do not want to hear any crap like that in this office again, do you understand??????"

"Yes Sir, Mr. Ambassador."

And we would continue.

"What was going on in there?," his secretary asked me one morning when I was making my exit.

"The Ambassador doesn't like the editorials," I said.

"So why do you tell him about them?" she said sweetly.

'I don't know," I replied. "I really don't know."

Political Ambassador? Me???

Because of his three Ambassadorships (he later added a fourth) under Republican Presidents, and because his manner was not, let us say, "careerlike," Ambassador Crowe was asked, not infrequently, by Norwegian journalists whether he was "a political ambassador."

"My country," he would say, "has three kinds of Ambassadors.

"We have some career ambassadors. Some are very good. Some are not.

"We have some political ambassadors. Some are quite good. Some are not.

"And my country also has a few distinguished individuals who serve their country, and their President, as ambassadors in time of need. These include Ellsworth Bunker, Henry Cabot Lodge, and me. I have always been prepared, when called upon by the President, to come to his service."

A much more indelicate question, which I saw him asked on two or three occasions, was whether he had made campaign contributions to obtain his Ambassadorship.

"I have never, ever given one dime to the Republican party," he would say, seemingly offended at the very idea.

And that apparently was the truth: it was his wife, heir to St. Louis' Brown Shoe Company fortune, whose generous contributions made possible what she called "Phillip's little hobby."

He loved "Ambassadoring." And she loved having him out of the house. Until Oslo, she had never once joined him at his posting. And when she came to Oslo ... and liked it ... well, this was not his idea of Ambassadoring.

Mrs. Crowe remained in Oslo for several months, and was still there when I departed. But sometime afterwards they were divorced, and Mr. Crowe took his Ambassador's hat to Copenhagen. He had long thought that it was there that he could do the most for .... yes, for the North Atlantic Salmon. Protecting these fish for his fellow rich anglers — the name of Prince Phillip was always dropped — was at the very top of his agenda. It seemed, as he told me several times, that the Danes were catching these wonderful fish in the open sea, and thus leaving fewer and fewer to climb, at spawning time, the rapids and waterfalls of wild rivers in Scotland, Iceland and Norway ...there to be caught by wealthy/distinguished gents. And the worst outrage — his face would turn ruddy when he told of this — was ....

"They even serve this salmon in TOURIST class on SAS!"

I was not the only one who never knew quite how to act, nor what to say, after such Ambassadorial pronouncements. I wasn't going to disagree, of course: for those who serve under them, Ambassadors, having their power from the President and the Congress, can not be wrong. Well, hardly ever.

The American Ambassador's residence in Oslo was, oddly enough, the largest of any in Europe. It had been a gift at some point of the Nobel family, and occupied all of a block in one of the city's fine old neighborhoods. It had a huge dining room and a huge dining room table. The table was not quite rectangular, but rather oblong. It could seat at least 30 and perhaps more.

Ambassador Crowe sat in the middle on one long side, flanked, generally, by the two ranking ladies. We minions — with my lowly press attaché rank I was always on the end — worked to make conversation with those on either side of us ... and generally to be inconspicuous.

"Inconspicuous" was of course not Ambassador Crowe's style. At least a time or two during the several courses we would hear his voice rising; hear him declaiming some often peculiar view, agitated enough to be heard the lengths of the table. All would grow respectfully silent.

One of Ambassador Crowe's claims was that he had been "on the last plane out" of Peking when (Nationalist) China fell to the Communists. I had no idea whether this was true or not ...but even I had by then met a half-dozen others who had also claimed to have been on this very last plane.

He was thus holding forth one evening ... the table being full of Norwegian Social Democrats (Norway's governments back then were always Social Democratic) ... and describing, loudly, the splendiferous stables in the Forbidden City. He described them in some detail: these had been built for the Emperor's horses, and they were very fortunate horses, indeed.

And then, his voice ever louder, and now commanding the attention of the entire room, and pounding his fist upon the table, the rhetorical question:

"And do you know what the Communists did to those stables?" he fairly shouted:

"They turned them in to a Goddamned public (BANG on the table) housing (BANG again) project!!!!!!!!!!!!!!!!! (BANG BANG).

I have no idea what those seated next to the Ambassador may have said at this point: one could hardly imagine a tirade more shocking to any good Scandinavian Social Democrat. Perhaps they sought to change the subject.

Down at my end of the table, there was simply discomfort. The Norwegians were too polite to comment. And I was simply grateful that no mere press attaché would ever be asked, in these surroundings, to explain how my Great Nation, in its Wisdom, having started out with Benjamin Franklin, John Adams, and Thomas Jefferson, now selected such emissaries.

Writing the Ambassador's Books

Ambassador Crowe published a book about each of his four "Ambassadoring" experiences: in Ceylon, South Africa, Norway and Denmark. I haven't said that he "wrote" these books. This, for example, is how a chapter on Norway's Lofoten Islands was put together:

As his "control officer" for this 1969 trip, I first wrote a long, long memorandum about the islands, their history, the economy and politics, etc. I then, as I worked out the detailed schedule, gave him another long memorandum about each of the hosts and hostesses he'd have on the four-day trip (during which we'd stay at the homes of local notables), and the other principal interlocutors whom he would meet.

Then, on the journey and before retiring each evening, I made extensive notes quoting, as faithfully as I could, every exchange he'd had ...and especially the most notable and quotable things he'd said. This was due on his desk three days after our return to Oslo. He did the cutting and editing himself. And this was true of every chapter ... And the responsibility of every trip's control officer.

Ambassador Crowe sometimes said that I too, should write a book. But I claimed to be put off by the requirement that all Foreign Service Officers get their manuscripts approved by the bureaucracy before going to a publisher.

"Nonsense, Bob," he said. "That silly rule applies to Ambassadors, too.

"Do what I do!" he commanded. "When the book's published I send a copy with a personal note to the Secretary of State. I then receive a polite note from him: 'Thank you, Phillip, for sharing your fascinating book with me.'

"After that, no damned bureaucrat is going to give me the slightest trouble."

Explaining Vietnam I

So I would go from Ambassador Crowe, in the morning, denouncing "Communists," to Norwegians the rest of the day, lamenting any number of America's problems of that decade: Vietnam, assassinations, racial strife, poverty, burning cities.

The farthest-left member of the Norwegian Parliament at that time was Torild Skard — who happened also to be the daughter of an important USIS contact: the professor of American Studies at the University of Oslo.

Among her other activities, Torild worked with Oslo teenagers who had dropped out of school and much else. One of her goals was to make them politically aware and curious. She scheduled two meetings for her group, both focusing on the war in Vietnam. The first was at the local Chinese Embassy. The second was at our Embassy, with me.

I prepared a show of my own slides. I was going to tell the kids how the Vietnamese that I knew actually lived, and what they aspired to. I was intending to appear to be talking to the teenagers but of course the perceptions that I wanted to change were Torild's.

When I wound up my talk, I was prepared for all of the difficult questions that we had to field daily about our war in Vietnam. First question:

"What time do Vietnamese kids have to be home at night?"

Second:

"What bands do kids in Vietnam like?"

I looked at Torild, and she just shrugged her shoulders. We passed the cookies and bade one another goodnight.

Explaining Vietnam II

You might think that The White House would answer its own mail. After all: every kid who writes to Queen Elizabeth II eventually gets a nice note from a Lady-in-Waiting.

But The White House apparently doesn't have the budget for such ... at least for mail which comes from foreign addresses. Those letters are screened for security threats, then sent out to the Embassies in the writers' home countries.

The letters from Norwegians to President Johnson, and then to President Nixon, eventually landed on my press attaché's desk. They were already weeks old when I received them. And they were never a priority for me, so many waited additional weeks before I responded.

And how does one respond to such letters ...when one is finally answering them, usually late at night after a long, long day?

Well: it can be tricky.

One letter, I recall, had been written to President Nixon's daughter, Tricia. The Norwegian girl who wrote it had apparently seen Tricia's photograph, and judged her a person with whom she might share a terrible secret: she had, she wrote, once stolen money from the cash register of a store in which she had worked. This had since troubled her conscience enormously. "What should I do?" she asked Ms Nixon.

Well! It was, of course, mighty tempting to write "My Daddy's Not a Crook!", signed "Tricia." I couldn't, of course, turn it over to the Norwegian cops ...nor could I think of any appropriate response whatsoever. So I never did answer it.

Most of the letters, though, were about the war — our war — in Vietnam. Most were critical, even condemning.

So the rare letter writers supporting us, I felt — there alone in my office late at night — should get considerable praise. If they were mildly supportive, I would say something like "Thank you", and enclose a pamphlet or two.

If they were quite supportive, I would say that "The White House has asked me to thank you ..."

And if they were very, very supportive, virtually mimicking our own rhetoric ... well!, those folks, I thought, deserved a special accolade.

"President Johnson (or Nixon)," I would write, "asked me to thank you for your insightful letter of support ...."

Only once did I ever hear how any of these letters were received. But when I was in Brønnøysund, one time, a small waterfront town just below the Arctic Circle, I was told that a local individual had been "going around for weeks waving a letter from President Johnson praising his wisdom and insight."

That individual was, I was told, "the village idiot."

I'm So Sorry, General Park

I don't know whether Norway's Nobel Prize Committee ever actually considered awarding the Peace Prize to Ho-chi-Minh (of course it did later, in 1973, award the prize jointly to Henry Kissinger and Lê-Đuc-Tho, Hanoi's Foreign Minister). But it was certainly very true that Norwegians, by a large majority, were, as the years passed, increasingly opposed to the war we were fighting in Vietnam. There were frequent marches to the Embassy by opponents; windows of the Saarinen-designed building were often smashed.

I was the single person in the Embassy who had been in Vietnam. And as Press Attaché/Information Officer, I was to be the point man on this contentious issue.

Although, after 18 months in the Vietnamese Delta, I personally had many reasons to question our policies (and actions!), it was also true that there was so little knowledge among Norwegians of what actually was going on there (most especially why millions of South Vietnamese dreaded and opposed a VietCong/Vietminh/North Vietnamese takeover) that I could often hope to end arguments by saying "Well: I've been there!"

Of course only a fraction of my propagandizing was face-to-face. I was also responsible for the "Daily USIS Press Bulletin" which was mailed daily (yes, this was pre-Internet!) to media throughout Norway. It went out in Norwegian, usually conscientiously translated by Leif Sommerset of my staff. But if Leif was away, the translation duties fell to our staff photographer, Per Rønnevik. Per, bless his heart, wasn't much of a news junkie — except for sports — and thus not infrequently made translation errors which amused, if not appalled, the few editors who actually read the thing. One day the very influential foreign editor of Oslo's Social Democratic daily, Arbeiderbladet, actually came to my office to point out a particularly egregious (and/or ridiculous) example:

It was a piece datelined Seoul, and included a reference to the then-President of South Korea, General Park.

Per had clearly thought this must refer to a park, like Central Park, in the Korean capital. He had thus forced the sentence to refer to "the General Park in Seoul."

Well: translating is tough. Although my Norwegian became pretty good through three years there, I was still often learning, when translating stories for the Ambassador or Washington, that all too many words had other, or at least additional, meanings than that which I had supposed.

Direct from the Lunar Landing (Almost)

(Note: the following ran, by-lined, in Norwegian, on the 40th anniversary of this visit, on the website of the Norwegian Space Center)

It was bizarre. Without telling anyone at all, I was supposed to arrange a very public visit to Oslo, only a few weeks after their July 1969 landing on the moon, of Apollo 11 astronauts Neil Armstrong, Buzz Aldrin, and Michael Collins.

The visit would eventually include a visit to the Norwegian Parliament, a chaotic motorcade up Karl Johansgata to the Palace, lunch with King Olav, and a discussion telecast "live" in Norway, Sweden, Finland and Denmark.

But from the moment when I was given the first cable telling me what was to be done, until the three arrived at Oslo's international airport on October 10th, all of these communications with Washington — with the White House, actually — were classified "SECRET/NODIS": not to be shared with anyone.

I have no idea why I — the Embassy's lowly 32-year-old press attaché — was given the job. One American secretary was permitted to do my typing and filing, and I presume that Ambassador Phillip Kingsland Crowe and/or Embassy #2 John Ausland could read the correspondence if they wished. But basically, I could not discuss the matter with anyone in the Embassy.

I found the confidence that I needed, though, in Tim Greve, then the splendid, capable and gentle chief of the Foreign Ministry's press department. The three Astronauts, their wives, and their party, would be arriving on October 10th, I told him, and leaving some 36 hours later. It was all "highly classified," I said. What should I/he/we do???????????

A much better diplomat than I would ever be, Tim first took responsibility for a very essential nicety that hadn't even occurred to me (or, perhaps, to Washington): "Of course we will invite them to visit Norway," Tim said. "They will be most welcome!"

Tim took charge. There would be schoolchildren waving Norwegian flags at the airport; the party would stay at the Grande Hotel; they would be received at the Parliament; there would be a motorcade to the Palace, where they would have lunch with King Olav, and they would do an hourlong Nordvision television discussion moderated by Norwegian Television's space expert, Erik Tandberg, and his Swedish, Finnish and Danish opposite numbers.

As Tim worked whatever bureaucratic magic he was working — with very, very few people in the know — I would do my cables to Washington: always SECRET/NODIS.

Three issues caused problems. One was finding a large convertible for the motorcade from the Parliament to the palace. This was "pre-oil" Norway: it was then a simpler, humbler place. What responsible and thoughtful Norwegian (and was there ever any other kind????) would possibly have owned an American-style convertible in 1969?

But a friend found one for me ... although I couldn't explain, of course, how it was to be (ab)used. Although its clutch started to slip when only halfway there, the convertible eventually reached the Palace entranceway, smoking considerably, but without failing completely.

The only dispute, really, was about the motorcade. There had been huge, huge crowds in the first cities which the Apollo 11 crew had visited. Excited and adoring, they had swelled into the streets, surrounding and sometimes even blocking the Astronauts' cars.

"That will never happen in Oslo," I was told. "Norwegians are calm, orderly; we obey rules.

"Even when Winston Churchill's motorcade took the same route after the war, there were throngs of admirers ....but we stayed on the sidewalks."

"THE CROWDS WILL EXCEED ALL EXPECTATIONS," Washington cabled. 'THEY WILL SURGE INTO THE STREET. THOUSANDS WILL WANT TO TOUCH THE CREW AND THEIR VEHICLE. YOU MUST PREPARE FOR THIS."

But Tim Greve's interlocutors, whoever they were, scoffed at this. Americans and Latins might behave so, they said: but Norwegians???? Never.

Washington was adamant. There had to be at least 30 police motorcycles. Most would start off behind the Astronauts' vehicle, moving forward to surround it as (and if) the crowd along Karl Johansgata reacted as no Norwegian crowd supposedly ever would. (As it turned out, even more motorcycles would have been useful.)

There was also a third issue: and the only one, actually, for which I alone found the solution.

Two days before the Astronauts' arrival, I sent the final ...and 54-page-long ... "SECRET/NODIS" cable to the White House, giving the choreography of virtually every minute of their Oslo stay.

In response, Washington had but one quibble: our super masculine astronauts were NOT to be subjected to the indignity of wearing pancake makeup in television appearances.

This was still the era of black & white television. Those appearing on it wore considerable amounts of makeup. "If they don't," Erik Tandberg told me, "they'll look pale and sickly ...and you don't want that, do you?" But Washington, when asked, said absolutely not: "NO MAKEUP FOR THE ASTRONAUTS. THIS IS IN THEIR CONTRACT."

But solutions can be found if one is (was) a bachelor press attaché. There were, in NRK's make up department, a trio of particularly lovely young ladies.

These three were told that they, alone among Norwegian women, would come within caressing distance of Armstrong, Aldrin and Collins. But they had a job to do: and they did it splendidly. Dressed that afternoon with the most enticing of cleavages, they virtually blocked the narrow corridor leading to the stage. Nor was there the slightest hint of objection from any of these very appreciative gents when the girls quite unexpectedly reached up and smeared their cheeks with powder puffs loaded with pancake makeup.

All went well. The trio, their wives and their party dined that evening in their hotel rooms ...while all of us who might conceivably have access to their quarters enjoyed enormous momentary popularity as folks begged and schemed for such entré.

Only ten more Astronauts would walk on the moon, and none have done so since 1972. A few more have circled it — including the Apollo VIII's William Anders, who became the American Ambassador to Oslo in 1976-77.

Anders, too, had visited Oslo not long after his own lunar journey, the first to circumnavigate the moon, in December 1968. I remember sitting with him on the terrace of the restaurant on Oslo's Holmenkollen mountain, looking out over that wonderful view of the city and fjord:

"When you see the whole earth the size of your fist, Bob," he said, "it's impossible to perceive our conflicts here on earth as you did before."

In a similar image, Craig Nelson wrote in Rocket Men that "at one moment, Armstrong realized that he could extend his fist and, using only his thumb, blot out the earth. Asked later if this made him feel like a giant, he said, 'No, it made me feel really, really small.'"

Forty years have passed. While nothing could seem lonelier than Armstrong and Aldrin bouncing strangely along the moon's surface, 211,000 miles from Earth, they were also, in those same moments, the singular focus of humankind everywhere. We were, at that moment, a single community. "People on every continent," Aldrin has written, "shared in our triumph as human beings."

When the Apollo XI crew departed, they left behind a clutchless convertible, thousands of snapshots, many stories ...and an exhausted American press attaché who would forever treasure a photo of an "earthrise" over a lunar horizon, taken by Michael Collins, signed by the three Astronauts, and reading:

"Bob ... Tak for Tur!" ("Thanks for the trip" in Norwegian.)

It was hardly a secret any longer.

My Windowette to Norway

My "windowette" to Norway was Margrethe. What she wasn't was as important as what she was. She wasn't an intellectual, spoke only Norwegian, wasn't a journalist or a politician or an academic; wasn't a sophisticate in any way. I had enough friends who were all of those, but Margrethe was my window to what I thought the "real" Norway.

She was raised as one of the some 1,200 inhabitants of the small island of Vega, a few miles off the coast, and just south of the Arctic Circle. Her father was a fisherman when Margrethe and I first met, but after the boat he crewed capsized and sank he became the community's chimney sweep. This, and his integrity, led to his being put onto the committee which oversaw the provision of assistance to the community's needy. "Because he's been in every home," Margrethe said.

Margrethe had had as much schooling as one could get on the island, and by ferrying daily to the middle school in Brønnøysund. But she'd done lots. For a couple of summers she had sailed with her dad and the crew to the Lofoten islands to take part in the famous, and huge, cod fishery there. While the men fished, Margrethe and another Vega teenager prepared the men's meals and took care of the small cabin in which they all stayed. She was thus also quite accustomed to managing in sometimes raucous male company.

Margrethe had cut and dug peat for heating. She was from a humble background ... but was, as everyone in Norway, assured a life of some quality by both the Norwegian welfare state and a strong work ethic.

When Margrethe and I spent a light-filled Midsummer night with her family around a glorious bonfire on a rocky promontory near their home, I felt myself as close to the old Nordic soul as an outsider ever could hope to be.

On this same trip the two of us drove northward and then eastward across the top of Norway, the Nordkapp, and through the Lappish/Sami highlands around Kautokeino., and then home via Finland and Sweden. Always Margrethe's observations, commentary, moods and embraces seemed wonderfully, refreshingly unaffected by whatever strictures I imagined constrained me and most with whom I otherwise associated. She even had a Sami friend in Oslo, an artist who also befriended me ... so that we traveled through the Vidda recalling his insights and tales as well.

We slept in a red tent on that northern trip — and fled into it as fast as we could when enveloped, as happened in this Vidda area, by buzzing swarms of mosquitoes. Hundreds would immediately swarm into the car whenever we opened a door. The only protection was a "mosquito spiral" which we would light in the tent ... once it was erected and our supper cooked.

Some of the Samis' faces were as covered by mosquitoes as I had seen Masai faces covered by flies in Kenya. In the Arctic, at least, frost would soon return (and thus be welcomed!). In Masai country there would never be any relief.

Back home in Oslo, Margrethe also shared with me her friends — individuals and groups that a diplomat, even such an oddball one, generally would not have come to know. I also learned something valuable from her brother, Rolf, who was deaf, mute, one-handed ...and very bright. I would never otherwise have spent so much time with such a non-verbal individual, nor have come to appreciate the intellect hidden behind such handicaps. Rolf was a champion bridge and chess player. Sometimes Margrethe would go off and leave Rolf and me together. We would take out the chess board and start a game. In about four moves, I would be hopelessly outmaneuvered. We would reverse the board. In four more moves, I would again be facing certain destruction. So we would reverse the board again. And again.

Sometimes, to make it just a bit challenging to him, he would play with his back to the board. But he had also done this against many much stronger players than I. He could also play several opponents at once this way.

Ever since, when encountering individuals who are non-verbal, I've wondered whether, as with Rolf, there functioned a considerable intellect behind the screen of their handicap.

Margrethe, with her humor and her flirtatiousness, got along well with my other Norwegian friends in Oslo. But there is a term in German —"salonfähig": "fit for the salon" — which conveys what my hesitations always were about bringing her into my "official" circles, as she did for me with hers. But we sailed on weekends with friends on a splendid 12-meter boat in the Oslo fjord, skied in the winter, and did the clubs. I don't think we ever parted having made a commitment to meet again. But it would always happen. I went out with many others, but the very absence of a leash from Margrethe kept me coming back to her again and again, including during my subsequent two years at Harvard.

Years later, when I was on a short visit to Oslo, she flew down from northernmost Norway to share a dinner together. As we laughed about old times, she said:

"Bob, if we had gotten married, we'd never be together here today ... or together today at all." And she was surely right (as well as a good many kilos heavier).

Some relationships should be short-term, and thus best remembered.

Grass Roots: New and Ancient

I was proud of the friendships that I'd made with Norwegians while in Oslo, including those with reporters, editors and producers that I'd dealt with as press attaché. Only 31 when I'd begun the three year tour, I had more in common with the reporters than with their bosses. But the editor of one of Oslo's seven (!) dailies became more than a professional acquaintance. And this became a friendship when, visiting the U.S. at the Embassy's invitation two years after my departure, he accompanied me from Washington DC to my dad's farm in the Shenandoah Valley to see what America and Americans were really like.

Arve Solstad's visit — this was in the spring of 1972 — coincided with the Presidential nominating convention of Virginia's Democratic party, at which the state's delegates to the national Democratic convention were to be chosen. The convention was to be in Roanoke, and my dad was chairman of the Augusta County Democratic committee. So Arve and I tagged along.

That was an exciting year: the year of the anti-Vietnam, populist McGovern insurgency. And Arve was intrigued. To their own astonishment (and it would lead to decades of diminishing Democratic power in the state), Virginia's Democrats — traditionally conservative to moderate, with a nasty racist heritage — rejected their leaders and went for the leftist McGovern. Arve thought that a lapel button sported by many of the McGovern delegates said it all: "I am a Grass Root."

Arve went back to Dagbladet, and Norway moved toward its referendum on whether or not to join the European Community, later the European Union. The entire Norwegian establishment supported a "yes" vote: business, labor, all but a couple of small political parties; virtually all of the media. With that sort of endorsement, a "no" vote seemed unthinkable.

But Arve had doubts. He sent reporters out to Norway's far-flung coastal and mountain communities, to the islands off the northwest coast, to the three provinces north of the Arctic Circle; to the women, farmers and old folks. "Report from the Grass Roots," said the headline over each such story. What people were saying in "the grass roots," the articles said, suggested that "no" sentiment was in fact quite strong and, outside of the cities, widespread.

The returns came in, and Norwegians had voted decisively to stay outside of uniting Europe. Only Dagbladet's reporting, of all the Norwegian media, had anticipated this result.

I dropped by Arve's Oslo office a few months later. He was still elated:

"You see, Bob," he said. "If you ask any Norwegian, anywhere in the country, where the word "grass roots" (grasrota) came from, they'll tell you that it's an old, old word going back to the Vikings, from the very start of Norwegian democracy.

"But you and I know differently," he grinned. "We know that 'grasrota' goes back to the 1972 Democratic convention in Roanoke, Virginia!"

Well, it was a splendid story, and I related it often. And then, nearly 20 years later, on a balmy evening in Copenhagen, I told it to an old Icelandic friend, Jón Baldvin Hannibalsson. I had known him in Iceland as the co-principal with his wife, Brydís, of a boarding school in the isolated Northwestern fjords. He had by this time been his nation's foreign minister for several years.

"'But you and I know differently,'" I quoted Arve as saying. "'We know that 'grasrota' goes back to the 1972 Democratic convention in Roanoke, Virginia!'"

But Jón Baldvin closed his eyes for a moment, tipped back his head, and recited, in Icelandic, an excerpt of a Saga.

"And so you see," he said, "'grasrota' <u>is</u> an old, old word going back to the Vikings!"

The Inspectors

Foreign Service posts are "inspected" every three or four years. A team of Foreign Service Officer colleagues, senior in rank to one's own post's leadership, arrives, spends a week to a month grilling everyone, checking every record, and measuring one's operation against global standards: i.e., Washington's expectations. Inspections are believed to have the potential to make or break one's career. They are preceded by months of preparations as the boss endeavors to bring the staff and its performance up to these Inspection standards.

I was a bit naïve about this when told by my boss, the Public Affairs Officer in Oslo, that our United States Information Service post in Norway was to be inspected. I'd served at three posts — in Finland, Somalia and South Vietnam — but had not previously been inspected. I thus didn't take entirely seriously Bill Astill's warnings and worries, nor share his apparent dread at what was about to happen to us.

I was the Information Officer, the Embassy's Press Attaché, and thus went through the Inspection "check list" comparing what we were doing in my department with what we were supposed to be doing. I made corrections as I could, and thought up excuses for those that didn't conform. But Bill's state of agitation grew daily as the Inspectors' arrival approached.

There would be two of them, both much senior to Bill, each very influential in our Washington DC headquarters, and each known to be very ambitious. Inspections were often (mis)used to push personal professional agendas, and Bill probably had good reason to be concerned.

But Bill was also something of a worry wart. So the Cultural Attaché and I each received multiple memos: pieces of paper, formal instructions, which would show the Inspectors, should we be found failing in this or that regard, that Bill Astill, our boss, had ordered us to improve and do it right.

One that I received had little (that I could see) to do with my performance at the office. Two Australian models had been living at my bachelor's apartment for some weeks, as Bill had learned from someone. His memo instructed me to get "these foreign persons" out of my residence. They could, he speculated, be a security risk.

How Carmen and Libby, both adventurous, lovely, and nurses as well as models, had come to live in my loft is another story, but neither the truth nor something that I might make up would have made any difference to my boss.

I had been told, in writing, that I was In Violation of something or other ...and thus, when the Inspectors learned of my transgression, it would be my hide, and not his.

I suppose that I might somehow have evicted these friends, even if temporarily. But there was no question but that the Inspectors would be coming to my home, dining there, and spending an evening there: checking every officer's quarters and how he or she "conducted representation" was a required Inspection exercise.

I discussed my dilemma with the girls, both long-tressed, shapely, mischievous and wonderful. Everything would be fine, they assured me. Just leave it to them. And I did.

The evening's guests were various reporters and editors: my "clientèle" as Press Attaché. There was probably a spouse or so as well.

There were the drinks, and the appetizers, and the buffet meal: all delicious and expertly prepared, and served by my two Aussie buddies. They could absolutely not have been more gorgeous. Nor cordial. Nor beguiling. Nor hospitable.

Coffee came, and cognac. Conversation flowed. In terms of "representation," it seemed to be a success. But what of my transgression?

The Norwegians left, in ones and twos, and then we were five: the two middle aged Inspectors, Carmen and Libby, and yours truly. How it happened, I don't know, but when I returned from a bathroom break each sofa held an Inspector ... and each Inspector's lap held an Australian.

It was, one of the Inspectors told me the next morning, "one of the nicest evenings that I've had in years." And having "foreign persons" sharing my digs was never, ever mentioned. A promotion came at year's end, but whether the Inspectors had anything to do with it I'll never know.

Off to Harvard

By my third year in Oslo my Norwegian had become quite good, and I probably could have asked for an extension for a fourth year. But my personal life was becoming quite complicated and, as had happened before, "fleeing" seemed the best option. But this became even more attractive when I was told by Washington that I had been selected to spend a year in "university training."

And this could be at any university that would have me. On full salary; moving expenses covered: the works.

Stanford!!!!, I decided. I'd spent only a single night on the West Coast: this way I could get my university year plus that supposedly unique California experience.

But I hadn't reckoned with my boss in Oslo, Bill Astill. I wrote my letter to USIA saying that I wanted Stanford and placed it in Bill's inbox for his required concurrence.

"Stanford????!!!" he asked incredulously; "Stanford???!!!!

"Don't you want them to take you seriously???? Is this some kind of joke? C'mon, Robert: obviously you have to ask for Harvard."

Bill Astill had graduated from Harvard College in the Class of '47, I think it was. He had then gone off to his first Foreign Service assignment, in Afghanistan, with the then-requisite china, silver and other niceties without which, he had been informed, a respectable junior diplomat in Kabul would not be taken seriously.

"You may not get Harvard, Bob," he said. "They may think you're only good enough for Stanford. But at least they'll know that you were serious about this university year."

And so it was: Harvard.

Harvard?! Me??!, 1970-71, 1972-73

Getting There

Harvard! Incredible, it seemed to me. I vaguely recalled having filled out only one application to graduate school, sometime after I'd put the Air Force behind me and before I went to The Chicago Tribune. It hadn't been done with much forethought, and I don't even remember whether I asked any Antioch professor to write me a letter of recommendation. Anyway, it was to Harvard, and to the history faculty. It was no surprise when I was turned down.

But here I was, in September 1970, at age 33, entering Harvard University's John F. Kennedy School of Government as a graduate student. With all of it paid for by Uncle Sam!

Several years later, in Bonn, some 20 of us, mostly Germans, sat in a circle in the living room of the political counselor of the American Embassy, Bill Smizer. We had all spent at least a year at Harvard, and we were now to introduce ourselves.

One after another, each gent noted the year that he had been there, the program that he had been in, and who had paid for it: always either the American, or the German, government. That had been true of me, too, during my first year in Cambridge: Uncle Sam had paid the tab. But I had gone back a second time, as a Research Fellow at the Center for International Affairs. So I was able to chortle, when I did my own self-introduction, that "Harvard itself paid for my year."

There was a murmur of respect from others in the circle.

But the fellow to my left, who was the last to speak, earned not only the most respect, but also a laugh:

"I was not a parasite," he said. "I actually paid my own way."

The Kennedy School Year

Spending a year at Harvard was something of a dream. Not a "dream come true," I think, since I'd only begun to think about such a privilege while assigned as press attaché in Oslo. But it was idyllic in any case:

Old Antioch friends Bob Yuan and Ed Bing were in Cambridge, as was Bob's lovely then wife, Ying-Ying. Ying-Ying found me a rent-controlled three-room apartment; they introduced me to friends through the year. My Norwegian galfriend, Margrethe, visited twice, for about a month each time.

In retrospect, I've often thought that I might have learned even more had I simply taken one course per semester, and audited others, as would have been permitted. But I lacked a Master's degree and thought I should earn one. This meant, to get the Kennedy School's Master of Public Affairs degree, taking four courses each semester.

I was a bit afraid of risking my grades on exams, so choose eight courses in which long research papers were required instead. I also chose courses taught by stars in their field: Daniel Patrick Moynihan, Seymour Martin Lipset, Stanley Hoffmann, Ithia de Sola Pool, and William Kaufmann (the latter two at MIT). I also took courses given by two younger faculty members: one on "Poverty and Inequality in America" by an assistant professor Weintraub, and the other, on "Transnational Relations" by Joseph Nye, Jr. Joe was later to become both Dean of the Kennedy School and a high political appointee in the Carter and Clinton administrations, as well as an outstanding academic.

He might also have continued to be a terrific mentor to young Bob Dickerman ... had Dickerman had any sense.

An "Opportunity of a Lifetime," Botched?

In any case, I worked harder during that 1970-71 academic year than at any previous time of my life. These were pre-word processing days: every one of these eight 80-to-120 page research papers had to be typed, both in draft and in final. In each semester I was writing four. The Trowbridge street apartment had a bedroom, and living room and a dining/kitchen area. The latter was my workshop. The books being used for each paper were in separate piles; each paper was drafted on a different color of paper. There were also separate piles of index cards. Often, exhausted, I would switch papers (and thus subjects and colors), and thus be reinvigorated for another hour or so. The subjects of the papers were completely unrelated. That for Professor Moynihan had something to do with universities; that for Professor Lipset something to do with intellectuals; and that for Professor Weintraub something to do with poverty in the U.S. There was a long paper for Stanley Hoffmann on Norway and the Common Market and one on nuclear weapons strategy for Professor Kaufmann.

One for MIT's Ithia del Sola Pool dealt with the way in which the Vietnam war had been portrayed by Norwegian television ...and thus how Norwegians' views about it had been shaped. Professor Pool was sufficiently impressed by this paper — it drew on my experience in both countries — to submit it to some sort of national competition of papers on "international communication." It didn't surprise me that no accolades were received in response.

But several years later, while running the American Cultural Center in Iceland, we hosted for a series of lectures by a professor of international communication at the University of Washington, Dr. Alex Edelstein. Alex asked if I might be the same Dickerman who had written that paper. He had been on the jury, he said: it had been "unquestionably" the very best of the papers they had considered. "But there was no way, in 1971, that a group of academics was going to give an award to a paper which might raise questions about their own perceptions of the Vietnam war."

The remaining paper, that for Joe Nye on "Transgovernmental Organization," actually had a result (other than the "A"s which all received). I collected my MPA (Master of Public Administration, but identified on my post-retirement calling card instead as "Minimal

Productive Activity") at the spring commencement in Harvard Yard, and moved to an apartment in Georgetown to become USIA's "Nordic Desk Officer."

I was called by Joe Nye at the office one day: how would I like to come to Harvard for a year, at Harvard's expense, and as a faculty-level Research Fellow, to write a book on "transgovernmental relations"?

I had impressed Joe with the paper which I'd done in his class on "Transnational Relations." In our first class session, he told us that he and Robert Keohane had worked for years on their book of the same name. "And if any of you can get us to change a single sentence in that book, you get an A." What I had written had led them to re-write a whole chapter. I accepted, and USIA agreed to let me go up on a leave of absence.

Harvard's Center for International Affairs, the "CFIA," was then still headed, formally, by Professor Henry Kissinger, although during his White House and State Department years he kept extending his leave of absence, never to return. It was a prestigious, prestigious place: I still have a hard time understanding why Joe Nye thought I was of that standard. My office mate, John Ruggie, went on to become chairman of the International Relations faculty at Columbia, and a renowned expert on the United Nations. John Yochelson, a buddy with whom I often supped, went to several major Washington jobs. There is a photograph of that year's CFIA Fellows. I suspect that every single one of them, both American and European, went on to a "distinguished" future. I might have, too, had I given Joe Nye reason to continue mentoring me; and/or had I done half as well in my CFIA work as I had in the Kennedy School year ....

But I was having trouble. First of all, I was belatedly realizing what earning a Ph.D. is all about. Lacking that training, and the analytical tools that it would have given me, I was constantly spending great effort trying to formulate thoughts for which the cognoscenti knew a well-trodden conceptual short cut.

Secondly, the academic "buzz words" with which I was working did exactly that: buzzed around in my overchallenged noggin, accompanied by the ceaseless whirring of the IBM Selectric typewriter. According to Joe Nye, I was to contrast the "asymmetrical dyad" of "transgovernmental relations" between Ottawa and Washington, and the "symmetrical triad" of "TGR" between Stockholm, Copenhagen and Oslo. And that was just the beginning of it. Nor could I, with my journalism background, imagine that anyone could possibly still be reading after page 35 or so.

The interviews in the five capitals, of course, were fun. Letters written on the letterhead of Harvard's Center for International Affairs gained me access that I would never, ever have had as a (non-Ambassadorial) diplomat.

There was an additional problem, and the most costly one. At age 36, I was becoming open to what in earlier years had been unthinkable: getting married. The problem was that I couldn't decide whether I wanted Norway or Sweden as my "country-in-law." I had met lovely, worldly, would-charm-anywhere Christina, who worked with Swedish Television's Washington bureau, during my Washington interregnum between the two Harvard years. We'd shared, for a while, a Georgetown apartment directly across N street from Averill and Pamela Harriman. She was much, much more than I deserved. But the alternative temptation of the monolingual island girl from north of the Arctic Circle didn't wane. The wavering through the year wasn't fair to either. Nor to Harvard. Nor to Joe. Nor to "the book." Nor to My Better Self.

But all was resolved by early spring. USIA had called to ask whether I'd be willing to head the USIS in Reykjavík starting in July. I accepted, told Joe I'd have to finish the monograph (no longer "the book") in Iceland, and asked how I should refund the remaining three months of my research fellowship. No one knew, of course: no one had ever before been so dimwitted (or so inferred my CFIA colleagues).

So under a huge oak in Harvard yard, witnessed by her mother and mine, brother William, and buddies Ed Bing and Vincent Perotta, Christina Lundblom and I were married. And off to Reykjavík we went.

And the monograph? Years later, in Bonn, I ran into an individual who had actually read it. It ran in International Organization, vol 30, number 2 (Spring 1976). Turgid? The introduction, drafted by Joe, set the tone:

"Eighty interviews with bureaucratic and political actors in five national capitals illustrate the Keohane/Nye theoretical argument concerning the importance of transnational factors in world politics. Focusing upon the development and application of integrative techniques ... the paper explores situations in which the demands of external and domestic harmonization are inconsistent and sometimes contradictory. The problem of maintaining 'dual coherence' in domestic and external policy and administration is identified ...."

Whew. And this took not only months at the CFIA, but many, many a weekend in Reykjavík. Academe has never tempted me since. Nor I it.

A Correlation

This isn't to say, of course, that the two Harvard years were not marvelous experiences. I left Cambridge better informed about global affairs, and better able to discuss them, than would ever be the case again. What if, I sometimes wondered, I'd gone on to a Foreign Service assignment where such issues might be paramount? Instead it was to Iceland, where Fish was what mattered most.

Of course: if, while in Norway, I'd become Bob Liv Ullman-Dickerman ....

But I learned very much at Harvard. I'd not been there long, for example, before I realized three things:

1) everyone was infinitely smarter than I was, and

2) I was the only one who smoked.

3) I wondered whether there might be a correlation.

But it was another two or three years of thinking about this before I finally quit.

Matchmaker

And there was some social life:

The other Foreign Service officer at the Kennedy School that year was Nick MacNeil, a State Department officer. I had old friends in Cambridge and he didn't. I took him along one evening to a party at Ed Bing's, an old Antioch classmate.

It was months before I realized that, at that party, Nick had met Bing's sweetheart, Linda ... and won her away.

Today, Nick and Linda are among the best friends that I have in Staunton. I've told their daughter that, were it not for me, there would be no her.

But when Nick asked me a couple of years ago to speak at his Kiwanis Club, I was quite surprised to hear him say in his introduction: "Bob keeps saying that he introduced me to my wife, but that's not true."

I did my talk, then asked Nick as we were leaving, "What did you mean that it wasn't I who got you and Linda together? Of course I did!"

"Well," said Nick. "I just think that you go too far when you say that you're also responsible for my kids."

Iceland, 1973-75

A Complexity of Memories

Of all the places that I'll be recalling here, it's the Icelandic memories which are the most complex; bittersweet.

No other years in which I lived abroad do I recall as frequently, nor as intensely, as those years in Iceland from 1973-75. I went to Reykjavík at age 36, newly married, just coming off of two heady years at Harvard, and being thought by my superiors in USIA to have a very promising future. I would be heading a USIS office for the first time. And I had chosen Iceland: it was a place which had intrigued me since my college year in Denmark, and had continued to do so through my subsequent years in Finland and Norway. It was the most Nordic of the Nordic lands. Washington had offered me the Icelandic posting when I was midway through my year as a research fellow at Harvard's Center for International Affairs. My colleagues at the Center could hardly conceal their incredulity that I was foreshortening my prestigious fellowship, and all that it might lead to, and even returning a portion of its money ... to go off to Iceland with Uncle Sam. And with a Swedish bride whom they had barely met.

That was in the spring of 1973.

But when Christina and I left Iceland less than two years later, I'd experienced the type of tension with my Ambassador which subordinates never win. It wouldn't help to learn, some years later, that he had been relieved of his second Ambassadorship after the intervention of the State Department's psychiatrist, for problems reminiscent of those we tried to work around in Iceland. Inevitably, the situation also impacted the newlyweds at home.

There was thus a good amount of bitter. So why are so many Icelandic memories so sweet????

Introduction to Iceland

We head for all countries with certain images of them. Iceland's included vague imaginings of Viking roots — of people, horses, cattle, sheep, dogs and a language, all of which supposedly had changed little since arriving from Norway a millennium early; of weather, and of a lunar, treeless landscape.

We met a single Icelander between the Harvard Yard wedding and departing. "How can you manage without trees?" we had asked, when he had shown us a photograph of his front yard in Reykjavík, with his parents standing proudly next to a shoulder-high birch which, he assured us, was — after having been carefully nurtured for many years — one of the city's tallest.

"Trees," he said, "block the view." And by the time that we left Iceland we understood: the view is the land, the sky, the sea, the geology: the whole wonderful, unobstructed 360 degrees of it. Trees just block the view.

The weather, people said, was what we most needed to prepare for: the knock-you-right-over wind (which would then come back and hit you from the opposite direction); the horizontal sleet that would blister through even the smallest opening in your clothing; the weather which changed every minute.

On the Saturday night of the first weekend that I was in our new seaside home — Christina was on a "saga" tour — the renowned weather arrived. Lumber from a nearby construction site flew past the window. Frigid gusts came through the triple-glazed windows. I foolishly opened the front door ...and was nearly sucked out. "If it's like this in late summer," I thought, "just imagine what a winter day must be like." And the raging continued well into Sunday.

At lunchtime at the office on Monday, my secretary, Thorunn Boulter, could not restrain herself longer:

"So, Robert, what did you think of the weather this weekend?" she said.

"Well, of course people told us about it. I suppose it was pretty normal," said I.

"Robert! It was a hurricane! We've been wondering when you were going to say something about it. We hardly ever have such weather!"

And yet ... it really was nothing, compared to the stories that we'd heard.

Innocents Abroad

We were so naïve! About marriage, about Ambassadors and Ambassadors' wives, about role-playing; about dealing with Washington, with subordinates, with relationships that blended the personal and the professional .... What weren't we naïve about?

We stayed at the Saga Hotel when first we arrived. An invitation had come to the office to the opening of an art exhibition. It was only a couple of blocks from the hotel. We walked over, found the address, knocked on the door, and were admitted.

A strange collection of people for an art opening, but what did we know? We hung our coats on a rack and proceeded upstairs. It was smoky, all male, rather dark ... and Christina, with her blonde beauty, was even more obviously out-of-place than I. I guess I asked one of the heavy-jowled gents about the art exhibit, no indication of such a thing being evident. But we had entered, as it turned out, a Soviet Embassy affair for the communist component of the Icelandic labor movement. We left: the first of any number of innocent mistakes which we would make in that strange, lovely, lonely land.

Within days of our arrival, Christina was encouraged by Dorothy Irving, the wife of our Ambassador, to join her and a number of other ladies on a multi-day bus tour through some of the sites of the Icelandic sagas. It would be led by "Magnus Scotti," a charming Scottish raconteur. Christina was delighted, and signed on.

The Irvings were to be our nemesis in Iceland. Christina was to get a foretaste of this the first night of the tour. All Icelanders go by their first names (there are no family names) and even among non-

Icelanders, on a bus trip like this, folks (non-German folks, in any case) would normally be on first-name terms from the beginning. But Mrs. Irving sensed a problem, and explained it to Christina:

"Because everyone on this trip is using the first names, Christina, you may also call me 'Dottie.'

"But of course when we return to Reykjavík, it will be 'Mrs. Irving.'"

"What is this?" asked Christina when she returned home. "If I'm to call her Mrs. Irving, shouldn't she call me Mrs. Dickerman?"

Nor was it the last time that my egalitarian Swedish mate would find diplomatic conventions absurd. Or, in the best case, just plain funny.

The Fish; the Base

It was an especially tricky time in a long-problematic U.S./ Icelandic relationship. The large U.S. military base in Keflavík, some 25 miles southwest of the capital, was a constant irritant. The governing coalition which had taken office in 1972, the year before, had pledged to have the base removed. And a year later the situation became much more complicated: Iceland had claimed sovereignty for 200 miles to sea, including rich fishing waters long harvested by British vessels. The ensuing "cod war" was no joke: not only were the transgressing (in Icelandic eyes) British fishing vessels being escorted by Her Majesty's Navy, but, in incredibly bad judgment, these same naval vessels were being supported by Royal Air Force planes flying out of the "NATO base" at Keflavík. The planes' mission was to monitor the locations of Iceland's two or three hardly-armed Coast Guard ships so that warships of the Royal Navy could confront them. In effect, the NATO base, supposedly there to protect Iceland, was supporting its "enemy" in this dispute over fishing rights. So it was a sensitive time.

Ambassador Fredrick Irving thus deserved the best support that he could possibly get from Washington, the military at Keflavík, and his small Embassy staff. Rarely had Iceland garnered as much attention and concern in Washington as then: this was the first and only NATO member with Communists in its governing coalition. And if the government succeeded, it would close the base and thus make impossible what Washington, and NATO headquarters in Brussels, considered absolutely essential: its capability to monitor, via air patrols and devices under the sea, the movements of the USSR's formidable fleet of nuclear submarines. These subs, sailing from the Kola peninsula, had to transit the depths between Iceland and Greenland, or between Iceland and Scotland, to roam the open Atlantic. On the list of U.S. strategic worries, few were higher than this: that we should be denied, in peace or war, access and "control" of this very strategically located piece of real estate.

While rarely foolish enough to actually take part in them, I had been witness at the CFIA to innumerable extremely sophisticated and complex discussions of international issues. I don't know, though, how those brilliant Harvard minds would have dealt with the peculiar challenges of this Icelandic/American/NATO "debate."

The base was located on the Reykjanes peninsula, on Iceland's southwestern corner. We wanted Icelanders to understand that it was there to protect Iceland against the Soviet Union and its Warsaw Pact allies. "So if you're here to defend us from the Russians, why isn't the base somewhere like Langanesfontur, on our northeastern corner????"

There was an almost insurmountable language problem: a cognitive disconnect, actually. For one thing, the whole system of apparati in and under the sea, of which the base was the nexus, was so highly classified that even its name couldn't be uttered. (It was SOSUS — the SOund SUrveillance System — and wasn't declassified until 1992.) So when we invited Icelandic parliamentarians or journalists to briefings in the base's war room, we had to focus exclusively on the base's aerial missions: the USAF fighters and the Navy anti-submarine aircraft, as well as its mid-Atlantic search and rescue capabilities. "See???? We really are here to defend you."

Another challenge was translating our rich (is that the word??) military and warmaking vocabulary into Icelandic. The Icelandic language is revered by the Icelanders, and defines their nationality and culture. But the country had never had a military, and the "warmaking" of the Sagas was of man-to-man conflict with often-flimsy swords and shields. A truly remarkable percentage of urban Icelanders ...our usual interlocutors ....were fluently multi-lingual. But the citizenry's debate, and its decision-making, were going to take place within the constraints of the Icelandic language. None of us in the Embassy spoke (or even read) Icelandic. One enlisted man at the base did. So influencing the Icelandic debate depended upon supporting those who already believed that Iceland's security was enhanced by this NATO presence, and hoping to provide them with arguments (and questions!) which they could then use with their more skeptical compatriots.

There was also the famous issue of the base's television. The base had had, long before Iceland established its own television, a low powered transmitter which broadcast taped American programming only (supposedly) within the confines of the base. But it was immensely popular with much of the capital's population, which (1) infuriated the "intellectual" and political left, and (2) caused many others to build, or order from abroad, antennas and amplifying devices which, in spite of the signal's weakness, enabled them to receive it across the 25 or so miles of lava fields between the base and the city. (Even when Icelandic television was up and operating, it telecast for only a couple of hours hours per evening, and — very sanely! — never on Thursdays. So the base's television had for several years been — until the Cod War — one of the most contentious issues in the bilateral relationship.

Before Ambassador Irving's time; before the forming of the coalition government which aimed to close the base, the Embassy and the military had supposedly done "everything" to keep the contentious signal within the confines of the base. But it continued to reach Reykjavík and its suburbs, to the relief of many but to the consternation of those who would "protect" Icelandic culture.

We sent young Vic Jackovich, my number two out to finally resolve the transmission issue.

It was, Vic found, quite simple: the transmitter had for all of those years been on the southwestern corner of the base, transmitting to and beyond it. We reversed this, and "base television" disappeared for good from Icelandic screens.

This caused an uproar — and raised questions within the center/left coalition about the political wisdom of actually carrying through on its campaign promise.

Among the "silent majority" who were so distressed to find their American television programming cut off was the grandmother of a good friend of ours: Ólafur Ragnar Grimsson, an assistant professor of political science at the University of Iceland. Ólafur was a leading member of the Organization of Liberals and Leftists and a member of the national broadcasting council.

"My grandmother is furious at me," Ólafur Ragnar admitted. "She says it was fine to talk about doing this ...but not to actually do it."

But the deed was done: and Ólafur Ragnar would go on to serve as his country's finance minister, and then its President. He is, in fact, now in his third term in that position.

"No Lefties ....."

Assistant Professor Ólafur Ragnar Grímsson was one of two Icelandic "influentials" (and friends!) whom Vic and I recommended for State Department-financed visits to the U.S. . This was the "Leader Grant" program. When invited by the Ambassador, these men and women — supposedly "rising future leaders" — received customized trips across the country, focusing on their own particular interests.

Ólafur Ragnar was one whom we recommended to Ambassador Irving for this program. Another was Vigdís Finnbogadóttir, then the director of the National Theater. Ambassador Irving vetoed both: "No Lefties go on this program on my watch," he said.

Vigdís was elected to Iceland's Presidency in 1980 and served until 1996. Ólafur Ragnar succeeded her. He is currently in his 3d term.

Vic I

Our staff in the Embassy in Reykjavík comprised only seven Foreign Service Officers, plus the Ambassador. There was a political officer, an economic/commercial officer, a consular officer, an administrative officer, the Deputy Chief of Mission and we two USIS officers, working across town out of our American Cultural Center.

My USIS #2, our "junior officer," was Vic Jackovich. Vic had been, we were told, the outstanding officer in his junior officer training course: "the very best" was to be sent to worrisome Reykjavík. And Vic was terrific: only a very few years later he was named our

Ambassador to worn-torn, constantly shelled Sarajevo, and then as Ambassador to Slovenia.

But Vic had had a rough start in his few weeks at the post ahead of my own arrival. Since the senior Icelander on the USIS staff, Ólafur Sigurdsson, was already ensconced in the second-best office, Vic was actually given a makeshift tabletop in the men's room! Then when Ólafur left, to be succeeded (albeit in a different office) by Hörður Bjarnasson, we both experienced the awkwardness of Ambassador Irving sometimes seeming to prefer to deal directly with our Icelandic subordinates rather than through us.

A few years later, Vic told me, he and Hörður met again, this time in Vienna. Hörður was at the point Iceland's Ambassador to Stockholm, Havana, the Holy See and several other capitals. Vic was our U.S. Ambassador to Slovenia. "We tried to pretend that we were big shot Ambassadors," Vic laughed. "But we knew we were just two blokes working for Bob Dickerman in the American Cultural Center in Reykjavík."

Vic II

Vic was also an accordion virtuoso. He'd had his own band while in high school in Des Moines. He could play for hours; every minute delightful: the accordion classics, semi-classical numbers, jazz improvisations either alone or in tandem with our young consular officer, John Tsacik. Christina and I loved it, taking advantage of him at every opportunity. And he reciprocated: getting fed at our house just as long as he brought his accordion along.

Our American Cultural Center was in a trim three-story building not far from the University of Iceland. The entire second floor was a lovely library. We loaned films on the first floor. The third floor had offices, plus a very nice reception room in which we held recitals, lectures and art exhibitions.

About once each month we brought from the U.S. a performer, artist, lecturer or expert on some area of shared Icelandic-American interest. These, with the library and the Fulbright exchange program, were our bread and butter: the means by which we sought to deepen the bilateral dialogue ...and to make more nuanced the often simplistic and undeservedly negative characterizations of Americans, the American nation, and American interests. I was particularly proud of the friendships we developed with Icelanders of the left and center left. It was here, I believed, that the fulcrum of Icelandic opinion rested. The Ambassador could, and did, engage the right and center right: Vic, Christina and I, and our USIS staff, facilities, and programs, would build the tougher bridges. It should be enough, I thought, to raise doubts about some of the conventional wisdom about "the NATO base." Would Iceland really be more secure without it???

Having the Ambassador at these discussions usually inhibited, I thought, this questioning. He wanted our Icelandic interlocutors across the spectrum to buy the whole package. I was concentrating on the Left (with whom, to tell the truth, I felt the greatest affinity). I felt it was enough to cause these people to doubt the wisdom of a simplistic we-can-do-it-alone international posture. Economically alone, the base was an important factor. Some 900 Icelanders worked there at one point; we were paying the entire cost of the country's only international airport, and Loftleiðer, the national airline, for which this was the home base, generated some ten percent of the national income. So there was much reason to question — without asking those on the political left to buy the whole argument of the right.

Vic III

One more word about the multi-talented, multi-lingual Vic Jackovich. His assignment after Iceland was to head (or was it to start?) the American Cultural Center in Sarajevo, the capital of the then federal Yugoslavian province of Bosnia-Herzegovina. There he fell in love with, and married, the daughter of a high-ranking officer in the Yugoslav army. This young lady was quite a character, and they were eventually divorced.

But years before that, I happened to visit them in their then-home in Falls Church, Virginia. I wanted, of course, to hear his wonderful accordion playing one more time.

"I can't," said Vic.

"Can't?????"

"R*** forbids it," he almost whispered.

It seems she had objected to his accordion from the very beginning of their relationship: "She's the daughter of a big shot Communist, and she considers the accordion a low-class instrument."

So much for the vanguards of the proletariat!

Liberating Our Troops One Woman at a Time

Since the Second World War the Icelanders, a country then of fewer than 200,000 inhabitants, had decreed a number of restrictions to minimize the impact of the large number of American servicemen on the country's small — and especially female — population. Enlisted personnel rarely had permission to leave the base. Officers could, but only in uniform.

Ambassador Irving was once lunching in downtown Reykjavík with the Icelandic Foreign Minister. An attractive female Navy officer, in uniform, came down the street. The Foreign Minister assessed her appreciatively.

"Beautiful," he said. "But why does she wear that uniform?"

"Because," said the Ambassador, "you require all of our officers to do so when off the base."

"But that's for the men!" said the Minister. "Not women!" (There being only one Icelandic word for a military person, hermaður and that was male: army man.)

Ambassador Irving returned to the Embassy delighted: this would dismantle a little bit of the firewall dividing the island's Americans and Icelanders. "Every little bit helps," he said.

But when he relayed this "order" from the Foreign Minister to the Admiral commanding the base, there was consternation; even outrage. In those years the U.S. military was only gradually learning how to deal with a growing number of female enlisted and officer personnel. But its orders were crystal clear: there was to be NO difference in rules or expectations for male and female personnel.

And now the American Ambassador had enabled female officers, but only female officers, to be spared the onerous mandatory uniform-off-base requirement.

One more friction between the Ambassador and the Admiral. And the former would soon order that the latter be replaced.

Oddities (Charms!)

There were so many oddities (charming peculiarities, actually):

Dogs were forbidden in Reykjavík.

Beer was forbidden in the entire country. (Although a small brewery in the northern coastal town of Akureyri produced lager which supposedly was exclusively for sale on the national airline, Loftleiðir. It was said that a remarkable number of cases somehow fell off of the trucks transporting them along the long drive south to the airport.)

Famously, bananas grew in a thermally-heated greenhouse in Hveragerði. For some reason this was a bigger tourist attraction than phenomenon which actually were unique to Iceland.

Bald golfers playing on the windblown nine hole course near our home in Seltjarnanes needed to wear caps: the resident seagulls loved attacking bare human noggins. (There is a midnight golf tournament on Midsummer in Akureyri, when, as for some days before and after, the sun never dips below the horizon.)

Just as there was no television on Thursdays, there were no newspapers one day per week (was it Mondays???).

The Icelandic ponies were famous for, among other attributes, being able to keep quite drunken riders aboard.

At a time of extreme inflation, tomatoes (also grown in the greenhouses) and paintings became more secure investments.

Icelandic babies were commonly put out on the balconies, well-bundled up, in freezing weather. The American infants at the base, who supposedly were outdoors only in brief rushes between quarters and cars, suffered quite a lot of respiratory problems. The Icelandic infants didn't.

As in New Zealand, there were many more sheep than people.

There quite unusual young diplomat at the French Embassy. He claimed to be the Embassy's "ski attaché," and he was as uncouth as they come. At a sit-down dinner at the French Ambassador's one evening, he wiped his chin with his necktie (the rest of us males were in tuxes) and explained to Christina: "I am an insult to Iceland's government."

Road-builders took into consideration places where elves were known to dwell, routing the roads around them.

The famous knitted Icelandic wool sweaters required some three weeks each to complete. In the 60's someone had displayed them in an event sponsored by Playboy. The resulting orders would apparently have required the total production of all of Iceland's knitters for a period of years.

One could watch whales being butchered and processed, mostly for the Japanese market, at a steamy, windblown outdoor plant in Hvalfjörður.

If every Icelander didn't actually know every other one, they'd certainly find a common acquaintance, or kin, within moments.

Reykjavík's swimming pools — one was just opposite my office — provided the opposite of a sauna experience: one sat, "cooking," in pools of various degrees of hellish heat, then lay in the freezing, blustering wind.

Since, Viking style, there are no family names (women are the <u>dóttir</u> of their father, men their father's <u>son</u>, a family of four might need four separate listings in a telephone book (which was alphabetical by first, i.e. only, name). In my family that would be daughters Anneke and Julia Robertsdóttir, mother Gerhild Hubertssdóttir and father Robert Charles(Karls)son.

The national legend has it that virtually all Icelanders today are descended from the original settlers from Western Norway ... as are the descendants of the sheep, cattle and horses that they brought with them. But a University of Iceland professor was, during our time there, doing the first genetic studies of the Icelandic population. As I understood it, a quite remarkable chunk of contemporary Icelandic genes can be traced not to the Norwegian Vikings ... but to the celibate (!) Irish monks who resided in caves along the south coast.

Of course there were more stories in this vein:

That the people of the Shetland and Færoe Islands "are descended from the Vikings who became seasick and couldn't continue the rest of the way"; and

That "the reason that the Icelandic women are so beautiful" is because the Vikings, returning from their raids, "brought home only the loveliest ones."

The Fun Side of Watergate

Having chosen a career in which I was, by definition, charged with defending, explaining, and rationalizing American culture, politics, policies and more, how was it, in 1974-5, to have to "explain" the unfolding Watergate affair?

It was a delight.

We were never asked to take the Nixon White House's side on this. We were encouraged, given the situation, to clarify, to "explain," the political, legal and Constitutional issues and procedures involved; to describe the stage, in effect, on which the ever-deepening plot(s) would play themselves out.

So that was rather fun. I remember how amused our leftist friend Ólafur Ragnar Grimsson was to read in Newsweek that President Nixon's income tax return indicated that he had taken a deduction for the table around which his Cabinet met! Did Ólafur, I wondered in later years, recall this when he became Iceland's Finance Minister, and then three-term President?

One of my "big bosses," Gene Kopp, came to Iceland at this time. Normally he would just have assessed the situation and evaluated my performance. Since he was a lawyer, a Republican political appointee, and the deputy director of the U S Information Agency, I had asked him some weeks earlier whether he'd be willing to speak to a class of students at the University of Iceland on the Watergate issue. He agreed, but came to regret this as daily new revelations seemed to put the White House in an ever worsening light. But Gene kept his promise.

During the question period a student asked: "What will you do if the President himself turns out to be implicated in this?"

"I would resign," Gene said.

He didn't, of course … and I never thought it decent to remind him of this when, in the summer of 1975, we occasionally met in the elevator at USIA.

Sami Sense

One often encounters, in such work, perceptions of the United States which are unexpected and, in this particular case, quite welcome:

Christina was working at Norduns Hus, the Nordic House in Reykjavík, a few blocks from our Menningarstofun Bandarikjanna, our American Cultural Center.

At one point the Nordic House brought to Reykjavík several Sami (Lapp) artists and cultural figures from Norway, Sweden and Finland. They exhibited their art, and shared perspectives.

A perspective that surprised me — one is of course "always" getting attacked for what white Americans did to Native Americans — was an envy, among the Sami, of the legal and cultural protections and the integrity which American tribes enjoy (if that is the proper word) on their reservations.

"When the Swedes wanted to build a huge hydro electric development on our reindeer grazing lands," one said, "we had no way to stop it. And since we have no designated territory of our own, we also, unlike your Native Americans, as I understand it, lack our own law-making and justice systems."

It would have been fascinating to send one or more of these individuals to the U.S. to meet with Native Americans and actually compare their relative situations. I indeed proposed this in a cable to Washington, Oslo, Stockholm and Helsinki. But in what was becoming routine, the Ambassador ordered me to withdraw the suggestion, and do a good deal of groveling to boot. He was a tough, even impossible, boss to please.

My Window into Iceland: Frank Ponzi

When Frank Ponzi died in early 2008, I wrote to his widow, Guðrún and their children, Margrét and Tómas, that no male, other than my father, had so influenced my sensibilities. A man of marvelous enthusiasms and terrific energy, Frank was a tri-lingual artist, writer, art historian, horticulturist, curator and fish farmer. And he had stories!

Stories about Joseph Hirschorn, to whom he had been secretary and advisor when Hirschorn was purchasing (often in bulk, according to Frank) the artworks which now form the collection of the Hirschorn Museum on the national Mall ...

Stories about actor and painter Zero Mostel, a buddy during that same Fifties period in Manhattan ...

Stories about Hans Richter, to whom he'd also been secretary, and Richter's fellow Dadaists ...

Stories about his neighbor, Haldur Laxness, Iceland's single Nobel Laureate, and their neighborhood ...

Stories about the English adventurers who traveled Iceland in the 19th century, and the illustrations and impressions that they brought home ... and

Stories of Iceland, of Italy, of the 19th century, and of New York.

Frank, a bespectacled Italian-American, and Guđrún, an Icelandic blonde, had fallen for one another when he was working with Richter at City College's Institute of Film Techniques and she was studying voice at the Julliard. Unlike almost all Icelandic-American couples, they'd decided to live in Iceland, not the U.S..

Frank's tale of shipping their few belongings from Hoboken to Iceland was one of Christina's and my favorites: we asked him to tell it again and again. Here it is as he wrote it in his 2008 memoir, DADA: Collage and Memoirs.

"After paying an entrance fee (actually a bribe), we accessed the Icelandic cargo freighter S.S. Trollafoss docked at Brooklyn's notorious "Red Hook" port. Our ship was scheduled to leave for Iceland on Monday. It was late Friday and we had driven down from Connecticut with all our belongings packed high on a trailer wagon. Because it was near the end of the workday we were directed to a longshoreman who took charge of storing possessions in a large caged-in area over the weekend. "Eh, ya don't tink your gonna still find these here Monday do ya?" was the threatening remark that greeted us. This came from a hulky, broken-nosed Brooklyn dockworker — the inference being another fee or bribe. As there was little to be had in Icelandic stores then, we were returning with crucial unobtainable home needs and some expensive items such as children's clothes, furniture, kitchen appliances, books and our own home-jarred vegetables and fruit. Our impatient, irascible dockworker was anxious to get home for the weekend. I quickly saw that he might be differently approached, so I redundantly asked if he was of Italian extraction. "Yea, so what?" was the brusque reply. Aware he was second Italo-American generation to my first, I knowingly asked "Can you speak the language?" "Nah, but I can understand it!" came the defensive response. Hoping to touch a common core, I addressed him in our mutually inherited old tongue. I explained how we, with <u>due piccoli bambini,</u> were returning with our sole possessions to Iceland to set up our first home. Hearing this touching tale of a young family with their small children, he turned to the other dockworkers ad shouted: "Heh! Dis guy's a real <u>paisano,</u> git his stuff in da cage!" Greatly relieved, I offered payment for his kindness and sudden change of heart. To this he reacted as though he had been stabbed, and mortally wounded. With upraised God-forbidding hands, he indicated that I had greatly offended him.

Then, taking me aside, he said that if I really wanted to help him, there was one favor I <u>could</u> do. "Sure, anything," I said.

"Well, when you git to Iceland; I mean when ya really git to your home in Iceland" he repeated, " Go into the church there and light a candle for my mother."

The Ponzis lived several miles inland from Reykjavík in a home they'd built themselves, starting at the bottom of a slope, and working upwards as they became able to afford additional rooms. Guðrun thus cooked in the kitchen on the lower level, where one entered, and would then carry the meal up two flights of stairs to the large living and dining room, off of which was Frank's studio.

Iceland was experiencing rampant inflation during our time there. With money of constantly decreasing value, Frank found financial security instead in tomatoes. The house already was connected to their own well of steaming geothermal water. He had since run these pipes into ever larger plastic-sheet covered greenhouses, where tomatoes grew profusely year-round. These he sold or bartered in town. When I visited years later, the enterprise had grown even more exotic: his greenhouses were producing grapes, avocados, herbs and more. He had also built fish ponds, now teaming with fish of all sizes. And there was a sauna, of course.

When we held art exhibits at our American Cultural Center, Frank hung the paintings. When our bi-national Fulbright board met, Frank chaired it. When I needed explanations for Icelandic behaviors, he provided them. When we visited their home, Frank regaled; Guđrun hostessed and sometimes sang; and Margrét and Tómas, perhaps 11 and 13 years old, would clobber me in chess.

I can never visit a museum nor art exhibit today without thinking of what Frank might be pointing out. Nor can I tend my tomatoes each summer without recalling his instructions in this regard. Nor, of course, can I ever hear opera without recalling the story of daughter Margrét, who was taking voice lessons from Guđrún, bringing with her one day her boyfriend Ólaf Órna Bjarnason, who played in a local rock band; of Ólaf listening attentively as Margrét performed her exercises, then asking Guđrún whether he might sing some of them himself; of Guđrún being so impressed (and surprised) that she offered to give him lessons as well; that he accepted ... and that he is today a frequently featured tenor in Italian and German opera houses.

West Germany, 1975-79

Bonn: Huge Pond, Tiny Fish

We had bought "The Farm" in Buffalo Gap while on leave from Iceland in January 1975. We concluded our Reykjavík tour in the spring and bought a small camper trailer which we placed in the farm's century-old orchard. The previous owners, Dr. and Mrs. Swink, were to remain in the house until the autumn. We thought we'd try the trailer in various locations, and thus identify the spot where we'd build a home. The first spot was at the western end of the "orchard ridge," looking eastward to Little North Mountain. The next spot was on the ridge's eastern end, facing the whole panorama of Big North and Crawford Mountains. That was the place. So although no new home was ever built, a successor to the first trailer remains at that spot today.

For six months we would both be studying German, albeit separately. We had rented an apartment in Alban Towers, catercorner from the National Cathedral on Wisconsin Avenue. (Having come from Iceland it never occurred to us to ask about air conditioning. There wasn't any. So clothes were rarely worn in that apartment.)

My German classes were at the Foreign Service Institute (FSI), in the Rosslyn area of Arlington, just across Key Bridge from Georgetown. We had bought a huge blue Oldsmobile convertible. Christina would be waiting in it for me when my class ended Friday afternoon. We'd drive, top down, to Buffalo Gap, spend the weekend there, then awake in the trailer at 4 o'clock Monday morning to head back to FSI. (This was the weekend arrangement which I very naïvely expected might be the family's when Julia and Anneke were growing up ...but "no 'way, Dad!")

We'd offered $60,000 for the 98.5 acres — without, I later realized, ever asking what the offering price was. Given the circumstances — it had been on the market for a year and both the house and the neighborhood were much in need of improvement — we almost certainly could have gotten it for somewhat less. But what did we know? There may never have been a couple as naïve about so many things as we. (This was also the year of the Great OPEC Oil Crisis, and its resulting inflation. We were offered either a fixed rate mortgage at 7% or an adjustable one. I chose the latter — and saw it soar to some 19% when we were in Bonn.)

We fixed fencing that summer, and occasionally cautiously entered the house to guess whether it was worth the maintenance work it clearly needed. Christina's German tutor was an Iranian lad: he came down one weekend and helped us with a floodgate, copied from Mother Earth News, which still hangs today, 35 years later.

Once, after we'd gone to bed in the trailer, accordion music awoke us. Dad had quietly driven over to serenade us. But this chapter, too, came to an end, and we were off to Bonn.

"A Small Town in Germany"

By 1975 Bonn had been the "temporary capital" of Germany for some 26 years.

It seemed likely to remain so for at least as many more.

Our Embassy was huge — one of the two or three largest in the world — and located in an inelegant six story building on the west bank of the Rhine river. The building supposedly had been designed to be a hospital — and was intended to finally actually become one just as soon as the two Germanys were reunited (if ever!). The Embassy lay on the left bank opposite the picturesque village of Königswinter, which was itself at the foot of the beautiful, Wagnerian Siebengebirge (Seven Mountains). A little putt-putt ferry boat crossed the river just above the Embassy. Another ferry was a couple of kilometers downstream, near the Embassy housing complex of Plittersdorf. My "commute" was the most beautiful that I ever had: bicycling along the

Rhine morning and evening in every season: the small family-crewed freighters with play equipment aboard and hanging laundry fluttering; the larger barges pushed by tugs; all, in multiple voices, plaintively tooting in the morning fog; the summertime cruise ships traveling between Rotterdam and Basel. I sometimes altered my commute, ferrying across to Königswinter, then biking past the vineyards on the right bank to the ferry crossing back to Plittersdorf.

The asphalted bike and pedestrian path along the riverbank continued into Bonn itself, then to Cologne, and presumably all of the way into the Netherlands. We sometimes biked into Bonn for concerts or shopping.

Less idyllic were the housing arrangements themselves. This was the only time in my career that I had to live in an Embassy, Americans-only, live-with-your-workmates housing situation. The Embassy had at least some 600 or so American staffers. Most had families. Most lived there in "Der amerikanische Siedlung." If you knew where an employee lived in Plittersdorf, you knew what his or her rank was. We lived on Martin-Luther-King-strasse, the top-ranking street (except for the Very Big Shots, who actually lived in houses).

I hadn't joined the Foreign Service to spend 24 hours per day with my compatriots, and was unhappy about this from the beginning. In an additional bit of bureaucratic insensitivity, we'd been assigned to a four-apartment unit immediately above that of my immediate boss ("Be careful not to scald him when you shower in the morning!") and across a landing from my boss' boss. It was unavoidable that we knew things about each other's evenings, nights, weekends, lives, marriages and peculiarities which really had nothing at all to do with our work. I'd leave the Embassy saying my hierarchical farewells to both Alan and John ...and then pretend just an hour later to be "just neighbors."

But even within an all-American apartment complex, there could be inter-cultural bemusements. My boss' boss' young daughter was visiting in our kitchen one evening as Christina was preparing to poach a salmon:

"What's that?" she asked.

"Our fish for supper!" responded Christina.

"That's fish??!!!!" she asked. "The fish my mom cooks are square."

Not My Preferred Foreign Service Work

In all the rest of my nine Foreign Service assignments, I was (sort of) "on the front lines." That, I thought, was why one chose this type of work in the first place.

Had I wanted to spend my life with my compatriots; had I wished to have a largely bureaucratic job, "I coulda stayed at home."

Bonn was the exception. For the first two years I orchestrated a flow of speakers and exhibits through our Amerika Häuser, our America Houses, in Hamburg, Cologne, Frankfurt, Stuttgart, Munich and Berlin, and to several bi-national "German American Institutes," themselves former Amerika Häuser in smaller cities including Tübingen, Heidelberg, Freiburg, Nürnberg, Saarbrücken, Bremen and Kiel. The Häuser were headed by one or two Foreign Service Officers, with USIS-paid German staffers. The Institutes ("GAIs") were run by binational boards of directors. Some were headed by FSOs, some by Americans on contract.

The Amerika Häuser had played a very important role in post-war (West) Germany's transition to a democratic federal republic. Two of the nation's subsequent prime ministers, Helmut Schmidt (1974-82) and Helmut Kohl (1982-98) described as "formative" the many hours they had spent, after the war, in the libraries of their local Amerika Häuser.

In many war-torn West German cities, in the late 1940's, the Häuser were in fact the preeminent cultural institution. In a history of the Amerika Haus in Frankfurt, its director from 1949 to 1955, Hans Tuch, recalled that "We had 23 staff librarians, we showed thousands of films, we had programs for children, and a parade of famous Americans including composer Paul Hindemith, actor Gary Cooper, writer Thornton Wilder and the Julliard String Quartet."

By the late 1970's the Amerika Häuser were having much-diminished impact, of course. But with a "successor generation" of Germans coming to adulthood, for whom the term "war" was more likely to be that in Vietnam than that which had destroyed their now rebuilt cities, we continued to fund, staff and "program" them. And it was, indeed, impressive that so very many prominent Americans were glad to speak at the Häuser for the $50 per day, plus per diem, which I was able to pay them, and that so many Germans continued to use our libraries, attend our programs, and view our exhibits.

And besides, no one wanted to close them. The individual German-American Institutes had evolved when we wished to close them, when influential local people resisted, and when, as a result, German federal, state and/or city funds were volunteered to fund what Uncle Sam said he no longer could.

So I spent my days on the phone with the various "field colleagues" and with Washington, scruffing up, scheduling and evaluating "programs." Christina, meanwhile, was again employed by Swedish Broadcasting, this time working for its Bonn bureau. We found few German friends, or even "contacts." And there was, in fact, a relative scarcity of federal officials in Bonn in relation to the many diplomats who wished to cultivate them. But it was a great place to take weekend trips from, and there was hiking and biking.

I found a way to escape these confines through the second half of my four year tour. Switching jobs, I became the supervisor of the American directors of the Häuser and GAIs in the south, and the Embassy's representative on the boards of directors of the GAIs in Heidelberg, Freiburg, Saarbrücken and Nürnberg. The good thing was that this often let me use a first-class, anywhere-in-Germany pass on the marvelous German railway system, including on weekends before or after astutely scheduled Friday and/or Monday "work" (yes, like Munich's Oktoberfest). The bad thing was that I was quite aware that I was not very good at this: my German was lousy; I was the supervisor of colleagues who probably deserved better, and I wasn't fitting in very well with my own bosses, back in Bonn, either. (To exaggerate just a little: if the GAI director in Tübingen, for whom I had enormous respect, had advertised a lecture program as "America: Best Country in the World?", both Jack and I would be asked "why the question mark????")

As in Iceland, where I also thought our efforts needed most to be directed to the "left", both intellectual and otherwise, I thought engaging skeptics by addressing provocative questions a better use of our time and resources than advocating to "conservatives" what they already were inclined to believe.

Hans Massaquoi, Liberian-German African-American

Of the many notable speakers whom we routed through the Amerika Häuser in those years — Paul Theroux, Allen Weinstein, Stanley Hoffmann and Fred Bergsten among them — none were more remarkable than Hans-Jürgen Massaquoi.

I would sometimes ask people: "What do you suppose is the mother tongue of the co-managing editor of Ebony magazine?"

The surprising answer? "Plattdeutsch," the "low" dialect of northern Germany.

Hans Massaquoi had been born in Hamburg in 1926, the son of a German nurse and the son of the Liberian Consul General. He'd thus been a mixed race schoolboy in the Nazi 30's, and a mulatto teenager through World War II. Denied, as a non-Aryan, the possibility of an academic secondary education, he had apprenticed as a metal worker. By the time he was 21, he had been witness not only to the racism and fanaticism of the Nazi era, but also to the virtual destruction of his hometown, Hamburg, to Allied bombing raids.

Previously a hindrance, Hans' skin color became an advantage immediately after the war: he befriended African-American merchant seamen, received cartons of cigarettes from them, and traded these for often-valuable items which now-desperate Germans proffered.

One of the many admirable qualities of Hans Massaquoi was that he had seen both the good and the bad in Europe, West Africa, and North America. He neither idealized nor demonized any of these three of his homelands:

From Hamburg Hans moved to Liberia, where his father and grandfather were people of high stature. Hans found their attitude toward their "inferiors" reminiscent of the Aryan arrogance he had known in Hamburg. "When my cousins and I would return home from evenings in Monrovia they'd kick the servants, sleeping under the house, awake and order them to make us a meal," he told me. He applied for, and received, a visa to study in the United States, and enrolled in an aviation mechanics school in Chicago.

In 1951, when the Korean War began, Hans received a draft notice (not realizing, until years later, that, as a non-citizen, this should not have happened). He became a paratrooper in the renowned 82d Airborne.

He returned to Chicago, enrolled at the University of Illinois' Chicago campus, and graduated in 1957. He joined Ebony magazine that same year, becoming co-managing editor ten years later.

Hans told me that, when he was still in the aviation mechanics school, he and a (white) friend, responding to a "help wanted" advertisement for metal workers, went to the personnel office of a Chicago manufacturing firm to apply.

"We filled out the applications, and waited," Hans said. "A while later the personnel director came over to us, reached for my friend's hand, and said with a big smile: 'Hans, we have the highest regard for German-trained metal workers. Welcome aboard!'"

"But I'm Phil," the friend said. "This is Hans."

"The man looked at me, turned around, and went back in his office," Hans said. "Soon the secretary told us that the positions had been filled."

Hans Massaquoi had many such stories, some of which he later included in a memoir, published first in English (Destined to Witness: Growing Up Black in Nazi Germany) and later in German (Neger, Neger, Schornsteinfeger! ...Black, Black, Chimney Sweep!) where it became a best seller.

But his subject, when he came to West Germany every three or four years to speak at our Amerika Häuser, was current developments in "Black America." He knew every leading person in African-American life: in politics, entertainment, sports, government, and academe. He would lecture in his native Plattdeutsch, drawing on the richness of his experience to convey a much more nuanced perspective on racial relations in the U.S. than one could have heard from any less extraordinary source.

Years later, when a quite-pregnant Gerhild and I were in Chicago, we accepted Hans' invitation to look him up at Johnson Publication's skyscraper on prestigious South Michigan avenue. (James Johnson, like fellow Chicagoan Hugh Hefner, had raised the funds for the first issue of his magazine by pawning several pieces of his mother's furniture.)

Hans showed us around: Mr. Johnson's huge office looking out over Lake Michigan, a whole floor of fitness equipment, the cosmetics company run by his daughters; the FM radio station also owned by the Johnson company. Hans also related the company's history: from the The Negro Digest, to JET, to Ebony and then its several auxiliary enterprises. He also told us the story of Mr. Johnson's acquisition of this impressive building:

"Mr. Johnson had moved his company through several buildings on the South side, but he always had his sights set on South Michigan avenue, inside the Loop. Working through a white lawyer, who wasn't revealing the identity of his client, the seller and buyer had settled on almost every issue.

"But Mr. Johnson hadn't actually been inside the building. So the lawyer explained to the seller that the buyer, in one final check, wanted his custodian to do a walk-through.

"The seller agreed. Mr. Johnson donned a pair of coveralls and took with him a plumber's wrench. He went through the whole building, room by room, pounding on the radiators and other pipes.

"And when he was finished, he told his lawyer to 'take it.' So he did."

"Even Their Slums Are Beautiful"

We all take our homegrown perspectives with us when we go abroad. Right?

And where do the rail lines generally run through American communities? Mostly through "the wrong side of the tracks" on both sides.

I was standing, with my mother, in the aisle of a German train. The window was down, the air fresh. We were going past one of thousands of Schrebergärten where German families garden small plots, and where they have often built small daytime-use-only sheds for tools ...and relaxing. The gardens typically grow flowers, berries and small fruit trees as well as vegetables.

"Even their slums are beautiful!" exclaimed my mother.

Finding Family

It had long been my understanding, before being assigned to our Embassy in West Germany, that, with one exception, our ancestors had been "bred and born" in the United States (and, indeed the Colonies) for generations.

That single exception was supposedly my father's mother, Adele Miller Dickerman, who had died of tuberculosis when her three children were still small. And now that I was myself headed to Germany, my father's older sister, my Aunt Virginia, suggested that I might be able to visit Adele's birthplace. She had Adele's German baptismal and confirmation papers, she said ...and now, finally, someone in the family would be able to read and translate them.

Aunt Virginia lived in Newport News and had a very low opinion of the general level of cultural awareness of burglars. She thus kept her valuables, including family treasures, in her piano bench. "Burglars have no idea that you can open a piano bench," she told me.

We extracted the two documents of Adele's from the piano bench. Sure enough: they were in German, and they were her baptismal and confirmation certificates. But even with my then-beginner's German, it was clear that these documents were not from a church in the Old Country, but one in Pennsylvania. Nevertheless, the papers identified Adele's parents, and the villages in Germany in which they had been born. I made copies of the papers and took them along when, in autumn 1975, we departed for Bonn.

Once there, however, I was unable to find either location on any current map. Not until my brother William arrived for a visit in 1978 did I take the papers out again. This time we went to the library of the geography faculty at the University of Bonn. And sure enough: in a historic atlas, there was one of the villages, albeit with a modified name, not far from the city of Kaiserslautern ...and the U.S. Air Force base nearby.

On a beautiful summer day we drove there in my old Volkswagen, curious to know from whence these great-grandparents of ours had emigrated. We drove over the crest of a hill and there was the village: neat, tidy, and apparently quite prosperous. As we entered the village we could note that the homes were substantial. Even the lanes into the meadows were asphalted. And parked in front of more than a few of the perhaps 30 homes were late model Mercedes and Audi sedans. Could this really be the village from which Adele's parents had moved to start a new and better life in America?

The village church was on a hillside on the opposite side of the village. There was a cemetery. Our great-grandfather's name had been Müller, changed to Miller in the U.S. , but our grandmother's mother's parents' surnames, Jung and Schwarm, were less common. And sure enough: all three surnames were to be found not only in the cemetery, but also on monuments to the village's fallen soldiers in the Franco-Prussian War of 1870-71 and World Wars I and II.

No longer doubting but that this now-prosperous village of Gogelhausen was that from which Adele's parents had emigrated, we drove back through it to look more closely. And now we saw something we'd missed before:

Parked by the barns behind several of the immaculate homes with the Mercedeses and Audis in front were other cars: older, rustier, grungier ...and with U.S. military license plates. The U.S. dollar was then at one of its low points in relation to the Deutschmark. A single beer, as I recall, was then costing nearly five dollars. And what was happening in this village, from which our great-grandparents had moved, was that American Air Force personnel from Kaiserslautern were renting off-base "quarters" in those barns. Thus the descendants of German emigrants to the United States, who presumably left to find greater economic opportunity, had returned to Germany ...and were barely able to afford to rent even very modest housing from the descendants of the villagers who had remained at home. So what if Adele's parents could have known this???

Promises Kept; Promises Broken

The outstanding Amerika Haus director during my time in West Germany was doubtless Ron Humphrey, in Cologne. Unlike some of our cultural centers, at which the programming had aged along with their audiences, Ron's Haus in Cologne had a vitality which attracted not only lively Germans in their 20's, but also German cultural icons of several generations. Ron Humphrey's Amerika Haus in Cologne, with its young, creative and fun German staff, was what we would have liked all of our remaining centers to be.

Ron and I found that we shared a commitment. We both felt that we owed our survival in Vietnam to a woman who had befriended and inspired us. We had both concluded our Vietnamese tours before the collapse of the Saigon regime. Both of the women remained in Vietnam; their families, livelihoods and indeed their lives endangered because of their years-long striving for a society better than that offered by Saigon or the Viet Cong, and their relationships with Americans, through whom they hoped these changes might eventuate.

International alliances are built upon complex webs of relationships and commitments. Presidents Kennedy, Johnson and Nixon pledged our country's commitment to defending the peoples of South Vietnam from North Vietnamese and communist aggression. Successive Secretaries of Defense and of State repeatedly made similar solemn pledges, as did successive American Ambassadors in Saigon and successive U.S. military commanders there.

In South Vietnam, webs of promises and reciprocal commitments descended to (and ascended from) the most basic grassroots level. Each of us "advisors," whether military or civilian, made such commitments to our Vietnamese counterparts; our advisees. Without our commitments, without our promises and our examples, could they really have believed that our risky joint endeavor would succeed?

Tens of thousands of lives, both Vietnamese and American, were "given" to keep these reciprocal promises.

At the level of chiefs of state, ambassadors, and military commanders, these commitments were institutional. But at the grassroots level — at the level at which Ron Humphrey and I had worked in the Vietnamese Delta — these commitments were personal. I owed my safety every day to my colleague Mr. Hiep's assessment of the relative safety of wherever we might be headed ...and, in turn, to those whom he trusted. And I owed my commitment to a better South Vietnam to the inspiration and example of Ms Huynh-thi-Tri and a handful of others.

It's surely easier to break an institutional promise than a personal one. Although both Lyndon Johnson and Richard Nixon fretted about the consequences of Vietnam being "lost" on their watch, I think it's fair to suspect that each was much more concerned about the consequences this would have for their political legacies than for any concern about the Vietnamese people, whether individually or collectively. How many thousands of American lives ... how many tens of thousands of Vietnamese lives ... were lost between the time that

Secretary of Defense McNamara, as he later acknowledged, realized that this war was unwinnable, and the time that we finally left?

And how else can we explain, other than his total lack of understanding and compassion, Ambassador Graham Martin's refusal, in the days just before the collapse, to permit any preparations being made to extract from the country the individual Vietnamese who would be most endangered because of their association with us????

Neither Ron Humphrey nor I were still in Vietnam when Saigon fell. But we both tried to keep promises we'd made because of the women to whom, we both felt, we owed our lives.

I recall sitting with Ron along the banks of the Rhine one lunch hour, probably in 1976, when he was in from Cologne. One of the Germans whose help he was trying to enlist to persuade the Vietnamese Communists to release "his" Nguyen-thi-Chieu was author Günther Grass. This had come to nothing, as did other such initiatives.

I commended Ron for working so diligently "to save her life as she had saved yours." In the case of Ms Tri, though, I was much less active or resourceful. I knew that further contact with me would only further endanger her ...and her husband and their two small children. I therefore simply encouraged my mother and others to try to be of whatever assistance they could, responding to her occasional very brief letters to them. When the "Orderly Departure Program" commenced in 1980, after I'd returned to the U.S. , Tri and her family applied for it. And then, for the next 12 years, I simply tried to keep their processing from being terminated, fouled up, messed up, mishandled and so forth.

Ron Humphrey, however, stepped 'way over the line. In mid-1978, when I was still in Bonn but he had returned to a job in USIA's "operations center," he was found guilty in federal court of having passed numerous classified documents, including two which were Top Secret, to a Vietnamese friend in the peace movement, understanding that they would be passed to the North Vietnamese delegation to the Paris "peace" talks. Ron was sentenced to 15 years in prison.

I did nothing, but wish that I had. There was no way that I could excuse Ron for having violated his trust as a Foreign Service Officer. But I did feel that somehow, amidst the "zillions" of promises which had been made by Americans to the Vietnamese since 1954, Ron Humphrey had been trying to keep just one of them.

I was vaguely aware that it sometimes occurs that judges, in sentencing, take into account correspondence from individuals citing mitigating circumstances. Israeli Prime Minister Benjamin Netanyahu did such a letter on behalf of his friend Tom Delay (!) in 2011. I think I might have shared a perspective on Ron which the judge might have taken into account. But I lacked the guts to "to the right thing" ...even while routinely condemning those who, in the 1950's, did less than they could have to defend victims of "McCarthyism." Ron Humphrey wasn't a victim. But neither was what he did completely without "honor." War is complex. And so are the relationships which it forges.

My Window to Labor: Joe Glazer

And now a word about perhaps my greatest (male) hero: "Labor's Troubador," Joe Glazer.

When Edward R. Murrow swore us in as the newest "Junior Officer Trainee" class of USIA in September 1961, all but two of us were in our 20's. We'd done a bit after college or grad school, but not much. Two, though, were "mid-career entrants": gents who had actually done things.

One was the incomparable Joe Glazer. Joe would become not only a good friend until his death in 2006 at the age of 88, but my entrée to organized labor in Iceland and West Germany.

When Joe had joined USIA, at the personal bidding of Edward R. Murrow, he had already been the education director of the Textile Workers of America, of the United Rubber Workers Union, and of the CIO. In France and the UK with the Marshall Plan after World War II, he had helped encourage and energize the non-communist labor movement. He had sung at the 1952 and 1956 Democratic conventions which nominated Adlai Stevenson to challenge Dwight D. Eisenhower. He had sung at strikes and rallies and with the burgeoning civil rights movement.

But I was probably the only person in our class who had known of Joe in his earlier incarnations. While still in 7th grade in Oberlin, Ohio, I had enjoyed listening to "The Singing Rubber Worker" over an Akron station. That was Joe. I also owned a 78 rpm record of his made for the CIO which, it turned out years later, he no longer had himself. I was proud to give it to him, just as I was proud while in Iceland to nominate him for USIA's most prestigious award (too prestigious to be awarded to Joe, as it turned out): that named for President Kennedy's USIA director, Edward R. Murrow.

American Embassies, in my experience, have a very hard time dealing with organized labor abroad. This is rarely a part of the backgrounds of our Foreign Service Officers. And in Republican administrations, particularly, there is simply a strong disinclination to engage with the "left," whether labor or intellectual.

But when Ambassadors, and thus their staffs, were willing, having Joe Glazer visit was a splendid opportunity to bridge this gap. Joe had actually been recruited to serve as a "labor information officer." Based in Mexico City, he traveled Latin America, singing for (and with!) the miners in Bolivia, the cane workers in Venezuela, the seamen in Argentina, the factory workers of Brazil and Colombia, and more. And of course Joe didn't just sing: he shared the stories of American workers, American struggles and American aspirations.

In the Cold War period, with the Soviet Union working through multiple front organizations to oppose American influence and democratic institutions, no battle was more important that that being fought on every factory floor, waterfront, and union hall.

During the Johnson and Carter Presidencies it became an annual event that our Ambassador to Oslo would invite to his residence virtually the entire (Labor party) Government, as well as many union leaders. I was never there for one of these events, but friends told of everyone joining Joe in lusty renditions of "The Mill Was Made of Marble," "Too Old to Work, Too Young to Die," "The Union is Behind Us; We Shall Not Be Moved", "We Shall Overcome," and more.

I was able to bring Joe to Iceland twice. We were in union halls in Reykjavík which may never have hosted an American. He sang for students, for trade unionists, and for intellectual "lefties" whom Christina and I invited home. (Two of these later became their country's President.) On a trip to the country's isolated northwestern fjords he charmed, and flirted with, blood-covered women in rubber boots during their breaks from filleting cod.

Our hosts there were Jón Baldvin Hannibalsson and his wife Brydís Schram, the co-headmasters of the local secondary school (which they had founded). Brydís was a famous Icelandic beauty as well as an influential cultural leader who would later head the Icelandic Film Institute during the years in which Icelandic films gained much international acclaim. Jón Baldvin would follow in his father's footsteps to lead Iceland's Social Democratic party. He would serve as Iceland's finance minister and then, for seven years, its Foreign Minister.

Joe of course fell in love with Brydís, as did every male who ever met her, and the couple were just as entranced by him. So after long day of singing in the fish plants and union halls, we'd keep Joe up into the early morning hours, drawing on his extraordinary memory of thousands of songs. My favorite times with Joe were these, when he'd do songs which might not have been appropriate, or understood, in his gigs as a cultural diplomat. Among my favorites were his songs of the Old Left: of Minsk and Pinsk, and of Socialists, Mensheviks, Bolsheviks and Trotskyites attacking one another in song. One such was "Our Line's Been Changed Again," taunting American Communists for bending whichever way Moscow ordered:

United fronts are what we love
Our line's been changed again.
From below and from above
Our line's been changed again.

We must appear to be sedate
Our line's been changed again.
The Revolution it can wait
Our line's been changed again.

We're now a party with finesse
Our line's been changed again.
With bourgeois groups we'll coalesce
Our line's been changed again.

We're simply communists devout
Our line's been changed again.
We're not sure what it's all about
Our line's been changed again.

Kaleidoscopic's what I mean
Our line's been changed again.
Now we're red and now we're green
Our line's been changed again.

In whatever country Joe found himself, he learned at least one song in the local language, and tried his best to do translations of a few verses of his usual repertoire. Adapting Woody Guthrie's "This Land is My Land" to others' nations was always a hit. In India the chorus became:

This land is your land, this land is my land
From Himalayas mountains to Kanyakumari
From the streets of Bombay to the hills of Assam
This land is your land, this land is my land.

I think Joe's third verse, especially, would have been applauded by Woody Guthrie:

I saw the Sikhs and the Hindus, the Christians and the Muslims,
From the plains of the Punjab to the Indian Ocean
I gazed at the faces of a million people
and I knew that this land was made for you and me.

When I brought Joe to Germany in 1979, I'm sure that I told him of my experience cutting sand paper in a Düsseldorf factory 20 years before. Having just spent a year at a Danish folkehøjskole run by the labor movement, I had expected all of my fellow Düsseldorf assembly line "comrades" to be Social Democrats as well. But it had turned out that most of them had fled from Communist East Germany and had had more than their fill of the "Left." Most were thus firmly in the camp of Konrad Adenauer's Christian Democratic Union.

But I was finding German trade unionism peculiar in the late 1970's as well. There was, for example, a huge strike against a key segment of West German industry by the nation's largest trade union, IG Metal. On each evening's TV news the head of the union and his industry counterpart were interviewed. Both were in well-tailored pinstriped suits; both were addressed as "Herr Doktor." Both spoke in a formal, educated, manner.

Someone had had the inspiration to survey a number of German workers, asking them which of these Herr Doktors was representing "labor." A sizable percentage couldn't tell!

But the program developed for Joe iby the Embassy's Foreign Service Officer labor attaché (a former music teacher who had probably never had a callus in his life) avoided such "Herr Doktors" and took him to actual work places. Joe considered the high point (well, low point, actually) when he performed for miners deep underground along the French border.

He returned, as he usually did after new adventures, with a song he'd learned down there. It was a great song for male voices, with a marching rhythm. Joe sang it for my staff.

"Joe!" they said. "NEVER sing that song here. Yes, it's an old German miners' song ...but the Nazis made it their own!"

The last time I heard Joe sing was here at the Buffalo Gap farm. He and his beloved wife and partner Mildred (he'd fallen for her already as a teenager) had been in West Virginia, the night before, "doing a gig at the nudist camp," Joe said.

But some months before that, Joe and Mildred had hosted a splendid dinner at their home in Chevy Chase, honoring our Icelandic friends, Jón Baldvin and Brydís. They had by then been Iceland's Ambassadorial couple for three years. We'd come full circle.

I owed dozens of friendships to Joe. As one far-left Icelandic trade unionist had once said to me: "Well, Robert: in spite of where you work, if you're a friend of Joe Glazer's you can't be all that bad." And it was in part because of Joe that, when Ambassador and Mrs. Irving hosted a large reception when we were leaving, we were told that "no one has ever seen this many leftists and labor people in this Ambassadorial residence." That made me rather proud.

Leaving Bonn

One of the several German Social Democrats who came to our apartment in Plittersdorf 1978 to enjoy Joe Glazer's songs and tales was, with her boyfriend, a slender ash blonde who had started, and was running, a mail order bookstore within Vorwärts, the publishing house of the Social Democratic party. It was hardly to be imagined then, but by the end of 1979, Christina and I had separated, as had Gerhild and her boyfriend; both of our fathers had passed away, and she was to follow me to Virginia some weeks after my Bonn tour ended. "Relationships" had proceeded very slowly, very hesitantly always before in my life. But not this time: Gerhild and I were married in Buffalo Gap on February 16th, 1980, and Julia arrived some nine and a half months later.

The Eastern Caribbean, 1983-85

To the Islands

It had never been my intention to be sent to a Caribbean island paradise ... nor, certainly, to seven such Eastern Caribbean nations ... and certainly not, while there, to work as hard and rewardingly as ever in my life.

Where I'd wanted to go in 1983, after a three-year Washington tour (and the birth there of both daughters), was to Denmark. I'd been hoping for years to eventually be assigned to the Embassy in the country in which I'd spent my junior year at Antioch.

The paperwork assigning me to Copenhagen wended its way through the USIA bureaucracy ... but was overturned in the Director's office, where his executive assistant put himself forward instead, and got the job.

Gerhild and I spoke about this at home. We decided that, the way things were going, this next tour might well be our last ...so why not go someplace, with Julia, 2 ½ , and Anneke, 8 months, like the Caribbean?

Initially, the job's only drawback — in addition to its "unpromotability" — seemed to be the obsession of the Reagan Administration's far-right wingers with an island ("that no one else had ever heard of"), Grenada, which they insisted was, with Cuba and Sandinista Nicaragua, part of the Western Hemisphere's axis of evil.

I thought I could manage that, given the beaches and the great amount of quality time there'd be with the daughters, and put in for the job of public affairs officer at the unusual "regional Embassy" in Barbados.

It wasn't until I'd been approved for the assignment, and it was too late to back out, that I learned, while being briefed at the State Department, that this Embassy was headed by perhaps the least qualified Ambassador that anyone had imagined — and one who "hated" the supposedly wimpish, callow and "leftist" Foreign Service.

One of the stories that Ambassador Milan Bish loved to tell — and I heard him tell it at a dozen inappropriate occasions — was of the call he had received, back home in Grand Island, Nebraska, from President Reagan:

"'Milan,' the President said: "I want you to be our Ambassador in Barbados.'"

"'B AR B A Y D O S?! Where in the hell is B AR B A Y D O S?????,' I said.

"And what the hell does an Ambassador do anyway?"

In any case, Ambassador Bish had arrived there some months before we did, and the stories about him multiplied. But it was also true that he was completely in accord with his ideological soulmates in the Reagan Administration who judged the New Jewel Movement government of Grenada to be dangerous "communists." (He had come to Ed Meese's notice when a leader in Nebraska, in 1980, of the "dump President Ford" effort.)

Ambassador Bish, and thus those of us on his staff, were accredited not only to the Government of Barbados (population 284,500, 2.5 times the size of the District of Columbia) , but also to six other tiny independent nations of the former British West Indies:

Antigua/Barbuda, 85,600 people; 2.5 times the size of DC

Dominica, 72,500; 4 times the size of DC,

Grenada, 90,700; 2 times the size of DC,

St. Kitts and Nevis, 40,100; 1.5 times the size of DC

St. Lucia, 160,200; 3.5 times the size of DC, and

St. Vincent and the Grenadines, 104,500; 2 times the size of DC

Our writ was these seven Afro-Caribbean, Anglophone countries, totaling a land area about two-thirds that of Rhode Island , with a combined population of something less than 750,000. But as I would sometimes point out, to the sputtering vexation of one of my Washington bosses: "I'm responsible for 20% of the votes in the

Organization of American States!" ...unlike my counterpart in Brazil (population 185,000,000+), for example, who could at most influence only 1/35th of the votes in the OAS.

So Gerhild and I had thought that this would be, except for "the Ambassador problem," a reasonably stress-free assignment, with plenty of quality time to relish on the two young daughters. Instead it turned into two years of long, sometimes chaotic 7-day workweeks, with me traveling in the other islands during much of the week, then having to catch up in my office in Barbados each weekend. And instead of being our last Foreign Service assignment, it quite unexpectedly gave me the challenge, exposure and promotion which led to my next and best Foreign Service assignment, as deputy chief of mission in our Embassy in Trinidad & Tobago.

But:

"My" Grenada: Ethics, Whistleblowing, Irony and Fate

The question was unavoidable: you've agreed to become an American diplomat; to represent your country abroad ...to represent your country's government abroad.

But what if your personal assessment is quite different?

We asked it when I was in junior office training, in the Kennedy administration. Twenty-five years later, new officers asked it of me when I headed the training division of the United States Information Agency.

There really wasn't a good answer. But among the possibilities were:

"Tough luck. You agreed to be Uncle Sam's mouthpiece abroad. If you can't do it, quit."

Or:

"So? You're a diplomat: you're paid to eat and drink for your country ... and to lie for it. So get off your moral high horse."

Or:

"The folks that make policy ... including this policy that you're having trouble with ... have access to lots more information than you do. So trust 'em ... and convince your interlocutors that Uncle Sam's view is the right view."

Or:

"So? Use your inside channels to affect the policy. You've got more influence as an insider than you would have as just plain Joe Citizen."

I suppose we all think that we have a pretty clear ethical standard: that, as the judge said of pornography, we'd "know it when we see it." And that we couldn't represent a view that we considered reprehensible.

But, in real life? ....

I had spent a couple of years in Somalia; serving in an all-White Embassy, telling Africans that racial relations in the U.S. were not as bad as they might think ("but nevertheless, my friend, it might be a good idea to wear that white Muslim skullcap so they'll know you're a foreign guest").

I felt that I was "explaining" ...not defending, nor "justifying."

I had spent three years in Norway as our press attaché. During that time "we" killed Martin Luther King Jr., Robert Kennedy and students at Kent State; burned Watts, Detroit, Newark and Washington DC; dropped more bombs in Vietnam than had been dropped in all of World War II, and defended our support of lousy South Vietnamese governments as critical lest other Asian "dominoes" fall to the Communists.

Again: I thought myself "explaining" ...and, since I'd been in Vietnam and few Norwegians had, I had some credibility. More, I supposed, than did Lyndon Johnson. And I had, after all, used those "inside channels" to make known my own perception of what was wrong ...not that it made any difference. And we surely now know that those of us in the field did, in fact, know much better what was going on than did our superiors in Washington. Or even in Saigon.

So 21 Foreign Service years passed ...doing my jobs in Finland, Somalia, Norway, Vietnam, Iceland and Germany, without ever having, QUITE, been driven to either quit in protest, or "whistleblow" a wrong.

Then, in 1983, I found myself in our regional Embassy in the Eastern Caribbean, responsible for the U.S. Information Service's work in seven tiny, independent, island countries.

One of these was Grenada ...population perhaps 90,000, and about twice the size of the District of Columbia.. The Reagan Administration ... and America's foreign policy conservatives ... were making very threatening noises about Grenada. It was a terrible threat to American security, it was argued. It was building an airstrip which, it was said, would be used to transfer weapons from the Soviet Union to Central America, and by the bad guys in Cuba and Nicaragua to fight (against South African forces) in Angola and Southwest Africa.

I was "uncomfortable," as we diplomats say, with this perception and this policy. I had visited Grenada soon after arriving in the region. It was clearly run by a group of young ideological hardliners, and more than a few presumably good folk were imprisoned ... but was this speck on the map really a "threat" to the American nation?????

And then, unexpectedly, some of the leaders of Grenada's government turned on others. Some were killed. And my job, as the Embassy's spokesman, was to say that the lives of American students at the local medical school were in danger.

The Embassy began bustling with people from Washington, both military and civilian. Numbers of mysterious aircraft assembled at Barbados' airport. An aircraft carrier and its escorts, on its way to the Mediterranean, were diverted in our direction. All of this was secret, but "emergency" Embassy staff meetings through the night made pretty clear what was underway: We were going to "liberate" Grenada, accompanied by a few score policeman and soldiers from Barbados, Jamaica, St. Vincent, Dominica, St. Lucia and Antigua.

I was appalled. I knew one person in Washington who might be able to stop it: a friend who was the staff director of the Senate Foreign Relations Committee. I called him. No one was home.

We attacked Grenada with bombers, Navy Seals, the 82d Airborne and a Marine Amphibious Unit. Nineteen Americans died ...mostly by friendly fire or accidents. We won. The Cuban "soldiers" of whom we had spoken so menacingly were repatriated through the Red Cross. The paunches on many suggested that they were, in fact, the "construction workers" which the Cubans and Grenadians had always claimed.

So I had tried to "blow the whistle" ... and failed. The United Nations condemned our action by an incredibly lop-sided vote. Every one of our European allies voted for the condemnation. Voting for our action: only our several island Allies, Israel, and the U.S..

But few in that United Nations majority, and few of those countries' leaders, understood Grenada, or the West Indies, or knew what the until-then-terrified, democratically-inclined peoples of those islands felt.

For the only time in my career, I was, when it became known in a store or a school or on a street corner that I was an American diplomat, stopped repeatedly while all around thanked and praised me profusely. This went on for months.

We had liberated the Grenadian people; freed them of a gang of hard-line ideologues and an army of thugs. People believed, sincerely, that Ronald Reagan was the instrument through which the Lord God had answered their prayers.

And would-be whistle blower Dickerman? I received awards and gained a visibility that had never previously come my way. I was promoted to the Senior Foreign Service, and given the best and most responsible job of my career: that of deputy chief of mission of our Embassy in Trinidad & Tobago. So what did this teach me about melding ethics with diplomacy? I don't know.

Liberating Grenada

Gerhild, Julia (then 2 ½) and Anneke (then 10 months old) and I were still living in temporary housing in a beachfront motel on Barbados' west coast when this several months of frenetic activity unexpectedly began.

The phone rang after we'd gone to bed one starry evening; the lazy surf splashing on the beach only a few yards beyond our door. It was our Embassy #2, Kim Flower. I was to be at a meeting at the Embassy immediately.

Three or four days earlier, on October 19, 1983, the self-described "Revolutionary" New Jewel Movement (NJM) governing Grenada had imploded. Deputy Prime Minister Bernard Coard, whom captured documents later revealed to be a committed Leninist of the Soviet/Cuban school, had, with his wife Phyllis and the Peoples Revolutionary Army, led a coup on October 13th against Prime Minister Maurice Bishop, placing him, drugged and tied to a bed, under house arrest. But large numbers of Grenadians demonstrated, and set him free. Before he could address his cheering supporters, however, Bishop was re-captured. He was then stood against a wall and shot to death along with seven others, including Cabinet members, by army troops. The Army then declared a four-day curfew, announcing that anyone leaving their homes without approval would be shot on sight. Even the Governor General, Sir Paul Scoon, was placed under house arrest.

As unexpected as this development was, there can be little doubt but that the Reagan Administration welcomed this opportunity to free Grenada of its leftist leadership. Conservative national security activists had long been beating the "imminent danger" drum about the 10,000 foot, reinforced concrete runway which the government was building with Cuban help (as well as that of the UK, Canada, Algeria and Libya). The Grenadians claimed it was solely to develop tourism. But Reagan administration officials argued that the strip's design indicated that it was actually to be used to refuel Cuban and Nicaraguan aircraft transporting troops to Angola and Southwest Africa, as well as to feed Soviet weapons into Central America. This argument was bolstered by the size of Grenada's Peoples Revolutionary Army — some 1,000 officers and men; trained and overseen by Cuba, which maintained a 40-man military training mission on the island. Small numbers of East German, North Korean, Libyan and Soviet trainers were also intermittently involved.

As several of us members of our Embassy's "Country Team" sat around a conference table waiting that night, for two or three hours, for anyone to tell us what was going on, the busy-ness in the corridor outside left but little doubt that something major was underway. We learned later that Washington had sent down, among many other officials, teams headed by two particularly senior diplomats. One was known to favor an immediate "liberation" of Grenada; the other was skeptical. But it would also become known later that then-National Security Advisor William T. Clark Jr. and then CIA Director William Colby had carefully managed their communications and decision-making in a way that excluded most all but a very few skeptical voices.

Meanwhile, CBC Radio in Barbados was doing terrific, 'round the clock coverage of the events unfolding in Grenada. Calls from terrified Grenadians were thus relayed not only in Barbados, but to Grenada, St. Vincent, St. Lucia , Dominica and Trinidad & Tobago as well. The regional wire service CANA, the Caribbean News Agency, also did terrific blanket coverage. (But both media, as well as the Barbados'two dailies, kept silent about the escalating number of U.S. military aircraft and military supplies parked in a corner of Barbados' single airport.)

There were thus at least three quite different rationales for sending military force into Grenada to restore stability: (1) responding to the urgent pleas of terrified Grenadians to "rescue" them; (2) the U.S.'long term, but through these days unstated, desire to rid the Caribbean of yet another government of the Cuban and Nicaraguan sort, and (3) the stated U.S. objective: to rescue supposedly endangered American students studying medicine at the island's St. Georges University.

Although several things went wrong — 19 American dead, none due to enemy fire; the mental hospital bombed rather than the army compound next door — what is remarkable, in retrospect, was how quickly the U.S. armed forces executed such an operation with absolutely no time for planning or exercising. Although conservative "intellectuals" in the U.S. had been relishing the prospect of removing what they viewed as the "threat" of tiny Grenada, the Pentagon hadn't even prepared maps of the island, much less game-planned invading it. A U.S. Navy Task force of nine vessels, including the carrier USS Independence, had been headed to Lebanon when it was suddenly diverted to command "Operation Urgent Fury" in Grenada. A tourist map of Grenada, published in the UK, was faxed to the fleet, then copied for the units preparing to invade by sea, plane, and paratroop drops. The 22d Marine Amphibious Unit was aboard. It attacked the picturesque capital town of St. George's and the island's east coast. Rangers parachuted into Point Salines to take control of the controversial airstrip. A large contingent of the 82d Airborne Division then followed, as did mountains of equipment and supplies ferried by plane from Barbados, the carrier and other ships. Navy SEALS and the supersecret Delta Force were involved, slipping onto the island ahead of the regular forces. The attack — the "invasion," the "rescue operation," the "liberation," depending upon your point of view — followed two days of bombing. It began at 5 am on October 25th. Within a very few days the number of troops on the ground was some 7,600, of which 353, members of the "Caribbean Peacekeeping Force," were our allies from Barbados, Jamaica, St. Lucia, St. Vincent and the Grenadines, Dominica and Antigua-Barbuda. Tiny Dominica's Prime Minister, Eugenia Charles, stood with President Reagan on the White House lawn that morning, announcing the "joint" action.

But back in Barbados I, and my USIS staff of one other American, Mike Morgan, and seven Barbadians, were the focal point of a huge media storm. Prevented by both the Grenadian coup-makers and the U.S. military from entering Grenada, some 600 journalists from around the world had now swarmed into Barbados, 145 miles to Grenada's east. Their producers and editors were demanding that they report on, and from, Grenada. But they might as well have been back in Miami, Washington, New York, Toronto, London, Frankfurt, Stockholm, Sao Paulo, Mexico City, Tokyo ....

"Washington" was adamant: it was to be the only source of news (statements, actually) about the Grenada action.

The newsies were furious: their editors thought they were in the war zone, but they had nothing whatsoever to report. Our USIS office was in a separate building a block from the Embassy, lacking the Embassy's impenetrable access controls. Our usual work, after all, was public: our library, our access. So dozens of newsfolk crowded into our space, setting up their typewriters on every available surface, and complaining, badgering and cussing. I was fielding one call after another from them, from my bosses in Washington, and from the Embassy. The latter two were especially difficult to manage, with newsfolk eavesdropping on every word. The calls continued around the clock: from Dan Rather, Barbara Walters, Wolf Blitzer and others. "I can't help you," I'd have to say. "Get your colleagues in Washington to beat up on the Pentagon." (And besides: how was I ever to have any information to impart when I almost never had a chance to ask any questions myself?)

I wasn't very impressed by this lot of newsfolk: and especially by the television journalists with their expensive haircuts and their inflated self-worth. Why, I thought, aren't they getting into local fishing boats and going over there? Only a half-dozen did so (three fortuitously arriving at the St. George's Careenage the morning of the invasion). But the rest simply complained and whined, so accustomed had they become, I thought, to being catered to, fussed about, and consequently beholden to, our Governmental handlers. (The enterprising three, in any case, did not find ways to get their stories out until all remaining resistance had subsided. One European journalist was reported missing. There was a great uproar from his paper, joined in by the otherwise hardly-busy journalists stranded in Barbados. The protests were vociferous enough to reach the White House. The Navy then admitted to holding him incommunicado aboard Admiral Metcalf's flagship.)

Three days after the invasion, the military opened the island to journalists, ferrying my Barbados flock over in USAF planes. Even the most cynical among them had to acknowledge the relief, jubilation and gratitude of the "rescued" Grenadian population. A small American Embassy was established in the capital, St. Georges. I set up an American Cultural Center in a former millinery shop. We hired three local staff and for a year or so sent American officers TDY, a month at a time, to head it. The military presence diminished week by week. The policemen from Barbados, Jamaica, Dominica, St. Lucia, St. Vincent and Antigua-Barbuda shared law enforcement duties with their Grenadian counterparts.

After having so often been on the defensive about American initiatives and/or conditions, it was quite a change to be, as an American diplomat, so very popular.

A couple of the St. Georges medical students, when landing at home, knelt down, Pope-like, to kiss American soil. President Reagan said that he watched this with "misty eyes." And a bipartisan Congressional fact-finding delegation, including several Members who had been outspokenly opposed to the incursion decided, after meetings with the leaders and other notables of the several participating island countries, that it had indeed been justified and welcomed.

Defending what we'd done fell instead to our Foreign Service colleagues in the one hundred and eight nations worldwide who voted in the United Nations General Assembly to condemn our action. (Eight nations voted with us: the participating East Caribbean nations, Jamaica ... and Israel.)

V.I.P. in a Very Small Place

Another recollection which would be quite unlikely anywhere other than the Eastern Caribbean:

When we shuttled speakers around the seven small nations for which we were responsible, we usually did so with the Embassy charter plane, affectionately known as "Air Banana." For some reason, when trying to take Professor Jiri Valenta to Dominica, we arrived at the Barbados airport after Air Banana had departed.

No matter: in those days immediately following the Grenada "rescue action" my budget was flush. We quickly chartered another plane, also with room for Jiri's wife and mine.

Jiri was a professor of political science and Soviet studies at the University of Miami, a fellow at the Woodrow Wilson International Center for Scholars, and the Coordinator of Soviet and East European Studies at the Naval Postgraduate School. Raised in Czechoslovakia, from which he had fled in 1968. He brought a remarkable background to the task of analyzing the thousands of Grenadian documents which were found/captured in Operation Urgent Fury. His book, <u>Grenada and Soviet/Cuban Policy: Internal Crisis and U.S. /OECS Intervention</u>, had just been published by the Wilson Center's Kennan Institute for Advanced Russian Studies. We had invited him to speak on his findings.

We landed on the frighteningly-short landing strip in Dominica a bit late, and hurried to meet the three individuals with whom we were to have lunch before Jiri's lecture at the small community college. I made the introductions (I thought) and we departed, in two vehicles, for a restaurant in the hills renowned for its "mountain chicken" (a.k.a. giant frog legs!). Jiri's attractive wife, Virginia, was also a scholar, focusing on Cuban policies in Latin America. She and the tall, balding Dominican gentleman next to whom she was sitting chatted animatedly through the lunch. She then asked him for his card, which identified him as:

H.E. Clarence Henry Augustus Seignoret

"What an interesting name!," said Virginia. "What does the 'H.E.' stand for?

"Oh," he responded modestly, "It's just for 'His Excellency.' I'm the President of Dominica, you see."

Where else could that possibly have happened?

"The Grenadian American (?)"

Within a month of the "rescue action," as we and most Grenadians called it, Washington had funded, and was sending the supplies for, an "American Center" in the lush, picturesque, rundown, capital of St. George's. I was to oversee it, while still based in Barbados, and it was to be staffed by a succession of U.S. Information Agency officers serving elsewhere in Latin America and the Caribbean.

One after another arrived, served, and left. I had rented a former ladies' hat shop for our library and office. There, each month, I hosted a reception to introduce the new temporary "director." These colleagues were both men and women, and both junior and senior.

At some point, the newly arrived officer was a fellow named John something — I forget what —a seemingly quite ordinary middle-aged Caucasian who, like most, had never previously been in the West Indies.

The Governor General and others were there: I made the usual introductions and the usual speech; the guests munched on cookies and enjoyed the wine. But several took me aside to tell me how remarkable it was that the new "director" "looks so Grenadian."

He didn't to me. All the Grenadians that I had ever seen were of various shades of black.

"Well," I said.

I went out afterwards with Alister and Cynthia Hughes, courageous local journalists who had, through the years of the New Jewel government and in spite of threats and harassment of all kinds, edited a monthly newsletter documenting the regime's violations of the rights and freedoms of the island's citizens.

"Cynthia," I said, "people kept telling me tonight that John looks like a Grenadian ...."

"Well," she said, "we thought so too, but it's not very polite to say so." And she explained:

"We celebrate, of course, the Wilberforce Act which freed the slaves in the British Colonies in 1833. But there were folks who lost their jobs when that occurred: the overseers; the generally poor whites who 'managed' the slaves for the plantation owners.

"A good number of these people remained on the islands after slavery had ended. There are small communities of them on several of the islands. In Barbados they're called "red legs." Here in Grenada, they're just Grenadians like us ...except that most live in the Mount St. Moritz area ....where they've been intermarrying for generations. So many of them are not very ....mmm ...smart. You see, Bob?"

"Well thanks, Cynthia," I said. "Isn't America wonderful?!"

Trinidad & Tobago, 1985-88

Running the Show

Somewhere along the line I'd begun to cultivate the conceit that I might be qualified to do more than run an Embassy's press and cultural activities. Much too realistic to put "Ambassador" as my ultimate career aim — as mid-level State Department officers were encouraged to do — I began to cite "deputy chief of mission", the number two job in an Embassy, as my career goal ...my fantasy, actually.

At that time only two or three U.S. Information Agency FSOs had ever been appointed DCM (as the State Department position was known). In each of those cases, I understood, there had been a career Ambassador who so wanted this particular individual that he or she had been prepared to fight the State Department assignment bureaucracy to get the deputy most desired. I was not known to any such Ambassador, and hadn't had a "mentor" either.

A Foreign Service "career" can seem a series of accidents: where one gets sent; for whom and with whom one works; the challenges — both foreseen and unforseeable — which one addresses; the "visibility" that does or does not accrue. There are many, many gifted men and women in the Foreign Service, and only a few duds. But the particular gifts which one has may not mesh particularly well with the requirements of a particular assignment at a particular time. And only rarely — if one does not have a mentor or two — do circumstances occur which can made a mid-level grunt suddenly shine, even in the shadow of superiors. In this work one is dealing with so much complexity: issues and tensions and frictions which may simultaneously be international, inter-cultural, inter- and intra-organizational, and inter-personal. Much depends upon serendipity:

I'd experienced the opposite of serendipity, whatever that may be called, in Iceland, working under a disturbed Ambassador whom neither I nor any other member of his staff was able to please. Of course the assignment itself was a mismatch: if I'd ever been prepared to deal articulately, in some capacity, with the most pressing issues of the time it was then, after two years of soaking up the wisdom and wit of some of the best minds at Harvard.

Lady Fortune made it up, though, there in the Caribbean. Utterly unexpectedly a beachside tour in Barbados became, because of a coup in neighboring Grenada, an event gaining global attention for days, national attention for weeks, and the attention of the Reagan White House for months. I was noticed by State Department chieftains who mentioned me favorably to the Ambassador-designate to Trinidad & Tobago, Sheldon J. Krys. And Ambassador Krys was that rare individual who, either because of great self-confidence or utter naiveté, was willing to chose his DCM sight-unseen.

So we were off to a quite different job, and a quite different country, only some 150 miles to the southwest. And instead of going through the usual sequence of "Washington consultations" and "home leave" between assignments, the four of us took a direct flight from an island in which we'd become quite well connected, to one in which we knew absolutely no one.

I'll always be most grateful to Ambassador Krys for having given me this opportunity. I learned much from him. And as it turned out, first because he was called away for various other duties, and then because of a several-month long hiatus between his departure and the confirmation and arrival of his successor, Charles Gargano, I was able to "run the Embassy" as chargé d'affaires ad interim for a total of perhaps 11 months. It was fun. And as mere chargés are notorious for doing, my speech at the huge Fourth of July celebration which Gerhild and I hosted in the Kryses' absence, was much, much longer than it needed to be.

A Nation in Transition

It was a fine time to be diplomating in Trinidad & Tobago, home to calypso, Carnival, "The Mighty Sparrow," multiracialism and 16 different species of hummingbird. A single party, the almost exclusively Afro-Trinidadian Peoples National Movement (PNM), had governed the two-island nation since 1962. In early 1986, however, a few months after our arrival, the PNM lost an election by a landslide (33-3) to a newly-formed party: the National Alliance for Reconstruction (NAR). The election brought significant numbers of Indo-Trinidadians into high governmental office for the first time. ("Indos" and "Afros" each accounted for some 41 percent of the population.) The PNM's aging, sclerotic and corrupt leadership was succeeded by a younger and multi-ethnic coalition. Several of the NAM ministers and members of Parliament, as well as a couple of High Court justices, became friends as well as professional interlocutors. A lovely home with lime, avocado, mango and palm trees came with the job, as did a full-time cook, housekeeper and driver. "Entertaining" thus was a very manageable challenge, and Gerhild orchestrated it with aplomb. And the girls moved, through those three years, from nursery school and kindergarten to an international elementary school, all beautifully multi-racial. Both work and life were rewarding.

The West Indies at their Best

The Presidency of Trinidad & Tobago was a largely ceremonial one. In the British model, political power resided in the Parliament. The majority coalition there chose the Prime Minister.

But the presidency had enormous symbolic value, and each of its presidents since independence had borne the office with dignity and honor.

The most impressive ceremony that I witnessed in Port-of-Spain ... and one of the most impressive I've seen anywhere ... was the installation in 1987 of a new President. The incumbent, Ellis Clark, was a distinguished Afro-Trinidadian who had held the country's highest diplomatic posts. He had also been the nation's chief justice.

For some Constitutional procedural reason the Presidency, in the ceremony that day, passed from Mr. Clark first to the President of the Parliament, and only then to the new President, Noor Hassanali. In doing so, power passed from a Trinidadian of African heritage, to one of Chinese descent, and thence to one of East Indian heritage (who also thus became the first Muslim head of state in the Western Hemisphere). It was often said of racial relations in that multi-racial, multi-faith land that one could argue whether, in terms of racial harmony, "the glass was half-empty or half-full." On that day, Trinidad and Tobago seemed to set a standard for all.

A Family Supper at the President's

President Hassanali was a most unostentatious, highly respected and dignified gentleman. A London-educated lawyer whose undergraduate studies had been in Toronto, he had retired as a High Court justice two years before being named, to his surprise, to his country's Presidency.

"We had moved to a small apartment in San Fernando," he told me, "and I had cards printed up saying: "Noor Hassanali ... no title, no job, no money."

President Hassanali and his wife, Zalayhar, were always most kind to Gerhild and me when we'd speak with them at the ceremonies and receptions which I attended as our Embassy's Number 2. But when the Kryses had returned to Washington, the Presidential couple invited our whole family — Gerhild, me, Julia, then 8, and Anneke, then 6 — to their residence for "a family supper."

"We didn't think we could do this when Ambassador Krys was here," Mrs. Hassanali told us. "But now that you're Chargé d'affaires I think it's all right."

It was sweet. They had wrapped small presents for the girls. The conversation was warm and relaxed. When the butler announced that supper was ready, we moved to a small table in their family dining room. More very pleasant conversation, absolutely non-political, and the girls behaved beautifully. After tea back in the living room we left, thanking them for a most unexpected and memorable evening.

Soon after we got home, Gerhild became violently sick to her stomach. When the vomiting and diarrhea wouldn't stop, we called the Embassy nurse late that night.

The meal at the President's had included chicken which had seemed a bit pink; a bit undone. For some reason the girls and I had declined it (perhaps not very diplomatic of us, but I think we had simply chosen other offerings). Gerhild, though, had eaten it.

The nurse, Faye Olson, decided that it was almost certainly a case of salmonella poisoning. She recommended moving to the private clinic just down our street. But we said that was unthinkable: the clinic would be required to report where a victim of salmonella had eaten, and what. And we vowed to keep that a secret ... until now.

Small Country, World Stage

In most years a country as small as Trinidad & Tobago (about the size of Delaware), with a population of only 1.3 million people, and politically and economically stable, would rarely, if ever, warrant any high level attention in Washington or at our mission to the United Nations.

In 1985 and 1986, however, "T&T" was one of ten non-permanent members of the United Nations Security Council. Although, unlike the five permanent members, it had no veto, it had one vote — as did, in those years, Egypt, India, Australia and others. We used our veto very sparingly. So on quite a few sensitive issues which came before the UNSC, Trinidad & Tobago's vote mattered.

For some reason, many of these occurred when Ambassador Krys was away. This meant that it was I who had to go over to the Foreign Ministry and present our demarches: our arguments, our urgings. Unlike State Department FSOs, who might have been delivering low- and/or mid-level inter-governmental messages for much of their careers, I, having been in "public" diplomacy, had rarely visited a Foreign Ministry on business. And there was a further handicap: I had of course never served in our mission to the United Nations, while each of my T&T Foreign Ministry interlocutors had served in theirs. More than a few times I went over with a démarche making points A, B, and C ...

only to be told by my interlocutor, in U.N. terminology that I barely understood, that 'Oh; that was the blue copy; now the red copy is being distributed, and there will be a yellow one" or some such.

Our Ambassador to the UN at that time was the inimitable, formidable, physical and intellectual giant Vernon Walters. Everyone knew that Walters spoke a couple of dozen languages ...but who knew that one of them was Trinidadian patois? Yes: his mother had been a British "colonial" raised in Trinidad, and during his upbringing in Europe she'd received the daily Trinidad Guardian. And he knew — and would happily recite — calypsoes from that era.

These family roots , though, were but one reason that he came to Port-of-Spain twice during his Ambassadorship at USUN. Another was Trinidad's aforementioned vote in the Security Council. And a third was the possibility of dropping in on the even smaller Eastern Caribbean nations. After all: they had one vote each in the General Assembly, just like everyone else. (The Ambassador to the UN of one of the smaller nations was, we understood, usually absent, plying his trade as a New York taxi driver. Two more were also only "part time." One of Ambassador Walters goals back then was to find the funding for a suite of offices which might be shared by the "delegations" from Grenada, St. Vincent, St. Lucia, Dominica, St. Kitts/Nevis and Antigua/Barbuda.)

Ambassador Walters was large. Perhaps nearly 300 pounds? In any case, I recall our limousine seeming to tilt to his side as we drove to and from a meeting with Prime Minister A.N.R. Robinson.

He kept working for Trinidad's Security Council votes when back in New York. A problem that we were having was that, after our meetings with the Foreign Ministry, we several times reported to Washington and New York that Trinidad & Tobago would, on this particular issue, vote with us rather than with the Non-Aligned Movement (NAM), as was their UN Ambassador's wont. Then the vote would take place; the Ambassador would once again vote with the NAM ...and we at the Embassy would again look incompetent and unprofessional.

I no longer recall which issue it involved, but one morning when I arrived outside Foreign Minister Mahibir's office to deliver our démarche, I was told to return right away to the Embassy to take a call from Ambassador Walters. I did so. Ambassador Walters was loudly venting about how important it was to have T&T's support on this ...and shouting what I should tell the Foreign Minister (and not necessarily in "diplomatic" language).

When I then returned to the Foreign Minister's office he received me graciously. Perhaps impressed by Ambassador Walter's personal involvement, he promised T&T's vote. I happily reported this to Ambassador Walter's office.

But when the Security Council vote was taken, Trinidad's Ambassador once again supported the Non-Aligned Movement position, causing immediate chagrin, embarrassment, soul searching ...and relief that Ambassador Walters didn't call to blame it on me.

Not until several years later did I finally learn what had been happening. On a wander through British Columbia I spent a day or so in Kelowna with the family of Sahadeo Basdeo. Sahadeo had become Trinidad's Foreign Minister after this Walters/UNSC period, but also living there was Ravi Persaud, who had been the ministry's political director during this time.

As Ravi explained it: Foreign Minister Mahibir, like Ravi, and like Sahadeo, was an Indo-Trinidadian. The country's long-time Ambassador to the UN, whose name I no longer recall, was an Afro-Trinidadian "of the old (to Hell with the Indians) school." Apparently the Foreign Minister was no less duped than we. Small consolation. Do things like this also happen with "big countries"???

Coming Home to Reality

It's important to try to remember, in diplomatic work, that much of the praise you receive, as well as much of the criticism, has little to do with you personally. If I'd been shot in Somalia or Vietnam, it wouldn't have been because I was Bob Dickerman, but because of someone's view of what I represented. Similarly, much if not most of the respect and honor which one receives is due, not to one's personal qualities, but to stature of the nation one represents. But remembering this can be a bit hard, especially when one nears the end of one's tour in a capital and is, almost always, feted:

The most flattering of the farewells thrown when Gerhild, I and the girls were nearing our departure date in Trinidad & Tobago was a black tie dinner hosted by the British High Commissioner/Ambassador. The guests, all in tuxedos and with their wives, included the Foreign Minister, the Finance Minister, a couple of Members of Parliament — all friends, actually — and my counterparts from two or three other Embassies.

As is customary at such affairs, one after another stood up and toasted us, lavishing on us great and hardly deserved praise.

We returned home, grateful and proud of ourselves. We parked behind the house and opened the kitchen door. Out rushed a flood of raw sewage. The kitchen floor was of two levels. The sewage, overflowing from a backed-up sewer through a toilet, had just about reached the higher of the two levels. This would have taken it into the rest of the first floor: the dining room, the living room, the family room ...

Off came the tuxedo and the long dress; boots went onto bare legs. We mopped and bailed for an hour or so before a plumber finally arrived.

By then most of the sewage was in the back yard. And any illusions of grandeur had been ... well: washed away.

Denmark, 1990-92

"The Happiest Country on Earth"

Denmark!!!! What a combination of wonders:

"The happiest country on earth," according to the Gallup World Polls in every year since the polling was first done in 2006.

The country with, according to the Heritage Foundation, the highest tax rates in the world;

The country with the highest percentage of women smokers;

The 13th wealthiest country in the world, in purchasing power parity, according to the World Bank;

The country with the world's 18th highest consumption of alcohol;

A country in which every employee receives 30 days per year of paid vacation ...plus holidays.

The country with the world's highest rate of working aged people receiving disability payments.

So how does all of this correlate? What's Denmark's happiness secret???

Several American Ambassadors to Copenhagen, all political appointees, assured their minions through the years that, given the country's tax rate, it surely would go bottoms up; and soon. But I've been going in and out of Denmark for more than 50 years. And it seems simply to get wealthier and wealthier, better and better educated, and more and more impressive and enviable.

"Interesting," as we diplomats are known to mutter.

"Dear Val ..."

My first visit to the American Embassy in Copenhagen was in 1957, when I was 20 years old. It was sort of down hill from then on. Let me explain:

When preparing to leave the U.S. for my 1957-58 year at a Danish folkehøjskole, I wrote a note to the only person I knew who was living in that country: the American Ambassador, Val Peterson.

"Dear Val," I wrote.

I would meet a half-dozen American Ambassadors to Copenhagen, either in Washington or there, through the next 44 years. But I would never again call one by their first name.

"Dear Val," I had written, recalling that I had interviewed him a couple of times for the Enquirer & News in Battle Creek, Michigan. Battle Creek was then the headquarters of Federal Civil Defense Administration (FCDA). A former three-term Republican Governor of Nebraska, Val Peterson had been named the FCDA's first director by President Eisenhower. It was also President Eisenhower who had named him to this Danish Ambassadorship. I wrote that, once I was settled in in Denmark, I'd like to come to the Embassy to do a follow-up story for the Enquirer & News.

"Looking forward to it," responded Val (short for Valdimar Erastus!).

And so it was that, in whatever my best foreign student/ folkehøjskole attire I may have had, I went into the Embassy, matter-of-factly told the Marine that Ambassador Peterson was waiting to see me, and was sent to his office on the second floor. "Val" greeted me heartily, showed me his office, and took me to lunch at his quite fancy club somewhere on the harbor. We returned to the Embassy; I thanked him, and I went back to Roskilde to write up my story.

That was the first time. The second time I was a mere lowly junior Foreign Service Officer en route from Helsinki to Mogadishu. I stopped at the Embassy not to see the Ambassador (God forbid!) but to speak with a USIS colleague on the ground floor. I don't know that my minion's knees were shaking, but I suspect that this time, when I spoke with the Marine, I was doing my most humble best: "Sir, Sir, Sir" .....

I was in the Copenhagen Embassy several other times before finally arriving at its front door as its new USIS director in December 1990. I may have been in the Ambassador's office once during that period, when I visited as USIA's Nordic Affairs Officer. Surprisingly, I wasn't invited there much more often when serving as, supposedly, the second-ranking FSO on the then-Ambassador's staff.

But who's to know? I'd fantasized for three decades about returning to Denmark as a diplomat. I'd be able to re-establish my years-long Danish contacts. And we'd be within easy visiting distance to Gerhild's German and Austrian families on beautiful Lake Constance. So it was Copenhagen.

The Copenhagen position was, though, beneath my rank; "below my pay grade." This virtually assured that, given the Foreign Service's up-or-out system, it would be our last tour. Confirmation of that eventually came — on the same day that, for the third year in a row, I received a $5,000 "meritorious performance" bonus.

In any case, the over-rank status gained for us a magnificent residence in upper crust Hellerup: seven bedrooms, a gorgeous yard, a magnificent veranda, all a block from the sound separating Denmark from Sweden.

But unlike our quarters in Trinidad, it came without "help." So Gerhild kept the girls and me, when downstairs, confined to the kitchen and a "family room." (We finally persuaded her to let us eat in this family room rather than the cramped kitchen.)

I was also seeing yet another Copenhagen. Through these three decades of occasional visits — never before as a resident, always en route from someplace to someplace — the Copenhagen I'd been able to experience (as in "afford"!) had been changing. When dropping in while a Scandinavian Seminar student, I could always find a sofa to sleep on at director Aage Neilsen's home in Vanløse.

The single time I actually took Elisa, my folkehøjskole love, "out", it was to an ultra cheap, but nevertheless barely affordable, Chinese restaurant in Copenhagen.

Somewhere along the line I learned of a "mistaken" room at the Royal SAS Hotel in the center of the city ...a room which was peculiarly shaped and rented out, cheaply, only to cognisanti like me. ("How do you know about that room?" the desk clerks would always ask.)

While doing my Harvard research, and several other times, I stayed in the city's Indramission hotels: clean, cheap quarters managed by religious folk who serve God by providing for travelers.

And in each new, better financed, incarnation, the eating and drinking locales changed as well, of course.

And now the fellow who, in 1957-58, would walk miles to avoid having to pay a trolley fare, was driving a car with a "CD" license plate (albeit bicycling to and from work), and raising his daughters in one of the poshest suburbs. From there we biked to Bakken, "the Danes' Tivoli," and explored the countryside. We took family trips to Bornholm, northern Jutland, Norway, Berlin and Bavaria.

But the location and ritziness of our new home was also, for me, something of an embarrassment. In my folkehøjskole days, Hellerup had been the notorious den of "the class enemies." Now I was living in their midst. Had I now become one of them???

Our Ambassador when first we arrived was the very genial Keith Brown ... twice chairman of the Republican National Finance Committee and (thus) twice an Ambassador; first to Botswana, and now to Denmark. As so often happened during Republican Administrations, the Embassy had lost almost all contact with the Social Democrats, the labor movement, and leftist intellectuals. Were these Ambassadors even aware that it was Social Democratic governments that had brought Denmark and Norway, after World War II, into NATO? Did anyone in these Embassies realize that, in the late 40's and the 50's, the battles with Communists were fought most importantly on the factory floor and in union halls ...by Social Democrats and free trade unionists? That Denmark's Social Democrats in every election received the greatest or second greatest number of votes? That competent diplomats should never permit themselves to become estranged from any significant sector of the nations in which they "serve"?

Ambassador Brown was succeeded by Richard B. Stone, a former Democratic Senator from Florida. Ambassador Stone eventually expressed an interest in meeting my "interesting contacts" ...but it was as we were preparing the guest list for Gerhild's and my farewell reception.

Danish Whimsies

Being one of hundreds of folks of all ages biking to and from work
The always fresh, slightly salty sea air blowing across the islands.
The hundreds of expensive, beautiful sailboats and motor launches

all along the coast from Copenhagen north to Helsingør.

Never forgetting what sweetheart Elisa taught me a half century ago on our strolls along the Roskilde Fjord: "Beauty is often in the smallest things."

The bicycling commuters on Fyn who supposedly, to always have the westerly wind behind them, might bike 5 kms eastward to work, then another 5 kms eastward after work, then take the bus 10 kms home again.

The quite possibly the most beautiful waterfront of any village anywhere: the view of downtown Æroskjøbing when one gets off the ferry from Fyn.

The quite possibly the most charming village anywhere: Gudhjem (God's Home) on the northeastern corner of the mid-Baltic island of Bornholm.

The delight that it was, before two huge bridges were built, to look forward to ferry rides if one was headed from Copenhagen west, to Fyn and beyond, or eastward to Sweden. But many small Danish islands are still reachable only by ferry.

The smørebrod — the open-faced sandwiches — of every delicious sort. The fish.

The breathtaking near-nudes, and occasional nudes, on any beach and along many a park path.

The gorgeous narrow streets of central Copenhagen ...and of the "old towns" of Odense and Aarhus.

The windswept Danish Færø Islands between the Shetlands and Iceland (where, it is claimed, "the Norwegian Vikings who got seasick got off.")

The occasional otherwise bewitchingly gorgeous young women in Copenhagen at whom, because of their grotesque facial piercings — eyebrows, ears, noses, lips, chins — I could hardly manage to look.

The oft-forgotten peculiarity that this otherwise small kingdom actually, with Greenland, extends from northeasternmost Canada to within 82 miles of Poland, and is thus one of the world's larger nations.

The friendliness. The good humor. The egalitarian values.

Hero Meets Boss: A Clash of Class

I might have known there'd be trouble when Ambassador Brown asked me: "What's NPR?"

"National Public Radio," I said. Ambassador Keith Brown, twice chairman of the Republican Finance Committee and a founder of Vail, was on his second "political" Ambassadorship.

"Hmmm," said he, apparently unfamiliar with that as well.

It was at an Embassy staff meeting. There has been a long tradition in Denmark, going back to 1912, of celebrating America's Fourth of July at Rebild, a Danish national park in northern Jutland. The tradition had been broken only two times, during each World War. The Rebild park had been given to the Danish nation by Danish-Americans proud of both of their heritages. The tradition had survived good times and bad in Danish-American relations, most notably through the years of the Vietnam war. When leftists in the late 60's had sought to close it down, supporters had rallied to the defense of "the freedom of the speaker's rostrum at Rebild."

But part of the reason for the event's longevity was that it had avoided, through more than eight decades, reference to "hard" policy issues. Messages from the President and the Queen were read each year. There was a prominent Danish speaker, who spoke in Danish, and a prominent American speaker, who spoke in English.

The choice of speakers each year was made by members of the "Rebild Committee," all Danes. Although virtually every American Vice President since Richard Nixon had spoken at Rebild, the committee actually preferred movie stars. They attracted larger and younger crowds to the event. And through recent years, attendance, especially of younger people, had dropped considerably.

I thought we had a chance to reverse these numbers that year. It would be the 45th anniversary of the popular Fulbright programs. We spoke with the staffs of the several high school and college programs linking Denmark and the U.S. . We hoped to have large numbers of these "kids" in the outdoor Rebild amphitheater, energetic and colorful with their banners and T-shirts.

Actually, Ambassador Brown's first question at that morning's staff meeting hadn't been about NPR. I had initially said that the American speaker would be Garrison Keillor. Ambassador Brown's

Rolodex included many if not most of America's rich and powerful. He had, after all, twice chaired the Republican Finance Committee. But it didn't have the name of my hero, "our time's Mark Twain" in my judgment: Garrison Keillor.

I thought I knew exactly why Keillor had been chosen. He had doubtless been recommended by the Danish Embassy in Washington. Gerhild and I had attended, a year before, a delightful lecture by Keillor at the Smithsonian. He had once been married to (and perhaps still was) a Danish redhead who had been an exchange student at Keillor's high school back in Minnesota.

The title of the Smithsonian lecture, which was both insightful and funny, was "Denmark: My Country-in-Law."

I thought Keillor a terrific choice, and said so. We went ahead with our plans. It was my USIS/cultural/press shop which had the responsibility for the event. Among the annual tasks: drafting the message from the President — then President George H. W. Bush — which would be read at the event on July 4th.

I used the traditional boilerplate "celebrating" our two countries' shared qualities and friendship. The cable with my draft went through the Embassy's front office for clearance. And when the "sent" copy came down to me it included a new sentence. This celebrated the two countries' participation just a few months before in Operation Desert Storm.

"Dennis," I protested to the Deputy Chief of Mission: "The Presidential messages at Rebild never get into such issues. This is not appropriate."

But Dennis Sandberg was a snarler. The text came back from the State Department, cleared by the White House. I hoped the potentially controversial sentence wouldn't be noticed.

The weather at Rebild was beautiful on that Fourth of July. Several hundred Danish and American exchange students, mostly teenagers, were there with their T-shirts, banners and high spirits. The highest ranking Danish official was the Minister of Education, who would make the "Danish speech." Ambassador Brown was there. Two or three dozen Danish-Americans from Texas were there. Garrison Keillor was there.

The Queen's Guard Band played both national anthems. Minister Haarder did the Danish speech. President Bush's message was read, including the line about Denmark and the United States having fought together in Operation Desert Storm.

Garrison Keillor, rumpled and heavy-eyebrowed, rose and spoke. About half of his speech was in Danish. He poked gentle fun at his "country-in-law," but clearly admired it greatly. He went back and forth between Danish and English. He praised international educational exchange, and the mutual understanding which it fostered. And then it came:

"Perhaps if we had better understanding of the Middle East, we would not have celebrated the killing of a hundred thousand Iraqis."

Ambassador Brown recoiled. So did the Danish-Americans from Texas. I rather suspect that a goodly number of the teenagers agreed with Keillor, but the atmosphere in the amphitheater suddenly chilled. Keillor went back to his more general theme, and soon was finished.

I thought it best to avoid Ambassador Brown and, especially, Dennis. Somehow I found myself alone in an area in back of the amphitheater's stage. And there, also alone, was Garrison Keillor.

"A very fine talk," I said. "Thank you for coming."

"Thank you," he said.

I said that, having been raised largely in the Midwest, I was a great fan of his.

"Where?" he said.

"Ohio and Indiana," I replied.

"Indiana's funny. Ohio's not," he said. And then a buxom woman in 19th century peasant garb inexplicably joined us. Keillor took her into his arms and they danced about.

The second part of the Rebild Fourth of July tradition is a dinner dance in a fancy hotel in Aalborg. It was black tie, as I recall. In any case, I didn't attend. But I was told the next morning that the atmosphere at the head table was frigid, with Ambassador Brown not deigning even to speak to Keillor, and Keillor thus rather isolated at that table of conservatives.

I found Ambassador Brown the next morning at breakfast. Seated with him were a handful of the Danish-Americans from Texas. They were telling him that Garrison Keillor was a "Communist," and that he should never have been permitted to speak at this event. In fact, they were almost suggesting that he shouldn't be permitted to have a passport .....

Keith Brown, though, was a gentle and forgiving soul. He said nothing about it to me.

At that hour I hadn't realized, nor perhaps had he, that Keillor's sentence about "celebrating the killing of 100,000 Iraqis" had made the front pages of all of Denmark's larger newspapers. Naively thinking that the story would die, I drove off to spend a couple of days visiting schools and cultural institutions in northern Jutland.

Back in Copenhagen, though, Dennis had stoked the anti-leftist tinder. He drafted an angry letter to Politiken, the large Copenhagen daily, denouncing Keillor's remark. The Ambassador signed it, and a conflagration of another sort erupted. I no longer remember the exact wording of the attention or the criticism. But none of it was supportive of what Ambassador Brown had done.

Of course I was supposed to be the Embassy's PR guy. But I was away, wandering in Jutland ...and neither Dennis nor the Ambassador had asked what I might have recommended (which would have been "Do Nothing!!!!!!").

I should have doubtless have mentioned by now, dear reader, that (1) Garrison Keillor had lived in Denmark for a couple of years and speaks quite good Danish; (2) his criticism of the recent "celebrating the killing of 100,000 Iraqis" — which he was implying we had done in the huge recent parades welcoming the troops home in New York City and elsewhere — also represented a widespread Danish view; and (3) neither a politician nor a diplomat should ever, ever get into a public fight with an astute and popular humorist — especially, especially when he speaks the local language and you don't.

The publicity and criticism went on for days. It also reached the American media. Each day I prepared for Ambassador Brown, and for Dennis, English translations of what was being said about us. To me the most devastating observation appeared in an editorial in the small Christian daily, Kristilig Dagbladet:

"Isn't it a tragedy," the paper said, "that through all of these years, including the Vietnam era, we Danes always defended the 'freedom of the rostrum at Rebild.'

"And now the greatest threat to that freedom comes from the highest ranking American official in this land."

I could say more — including how awful I felt when having had to invite two or three Danish editors, including that of Kristelig

Dagbladet, to meet with Dennis, and there to witness them being excoriated not by my "political Ambassador," but my fellow Foreign Service Officer.

More than a decade later, I was phoned at the farm in Buffalo Gap by a man whose name I didn't catch. He was calling to praise a letter to the editor I'd written which had denounced one or another position of our ultra-conservative Congressman, Bob Goodlatte.

Eventually I put "Middlebrooke" and "Robin" together and realized that my caller must be local musician Robin Williams who, with his wife Linda, appear very frequently with Garrison Keillor on "Prairie Home Companion."

I suppose I instantly became a Groupie, both embarrassed and flattered to be called by such a person. And of course I had to tell him this story.

"I'd heard it from him," Robin said.

"Tell him; tell him; tell him please that I apologize so much for what occurred there in Denmark. And that Garrison Keillor is my folk hero."

More years passed. And eventually Garrison Keillor came to Staunton to sing and tell stories at Robin and Linda Williams'annual music festival.

I went up to him, recalled the Rebild episode, and said I wanted to apologize for "my Ambassador."

"That's okay," he said genially. "Besides, he was my Ambassador, not yours."

In some of his interviews in Copenhagen during the episode, Keillor had said that he would be portraying Ambassador Brown in "Prairie Home" sometime after he returned.

I'm not aware that he ever did. So now you have the story, from me.

In Costume for the Queen

Every capital has its own traditions — or, at least, procedures — by which new Ambassadors, the representatives "Extraordinary and Plenipotentiary" of their own sovereigns, formally present their credentials to the host country's Chief of State. In Washington, DC, in recognition of the many demands upon the President's time, these are generally group affairs. In older countries, including Denmark, some of the formality that characterized inter-state diplomacy centuries ago continues today.

When our new Ambassador to Copenhagen, former Florida Senator Richard Stone, was to present his credentials to Queen Margrethe II, the procedure was: (1) Ambassador and Mrs. Stone were picked up in front of our Embassy by a horse-drawn royal coach; while (2) the Ambassador's two ranking diplomats and his military attaché arrived at Amalienborg Palace separately in an Embassy vehicle. All three of us civilian gents — Ambassador Stone, Deputy Chief of Mission Dennis Sandberg and I — were to be dressed in formal evening dress: a black "tailcoat" with silk facings; "fish-tail" black trousers with two satin stripes, held up not by a belt but by braces; a white, stiff-fronted shirt with a separate white stiff-winged collar; a white low-cut vest, white gloves, long black socks and black pants.

A high-crowned opera (or "top") hat was also required.

Not, obviously, what every working stiff diplomat today travels around with. Or in.

So where did one rent such attire in Copenhagen? At a costume shop on Vesterbrogade, near the train station and the "porno street." Dennis and I went together. And there, in one corner upstairs, was what we needed ... right next to the Giant Gorilla, Wonder Woman and Miss Piggy costumes.

At precisely the appointed minute, we were escorted into the room where Her Majesty, herself a noted artist and costume designer, sat demurely. She exchanged several pleasantries with the Stones, then asked each of us underlings a polite question. Naturally, I had to respond in Danish that I'd studied years before at Denmark's "workers folk high school" in Roskilde. "How interesting," she said, as if she had understood, and we were dismissed.

By the time we reconvened a bit later for celebratory champagne in the Ambassador's office, I had replaced the elegant opera hat with the somewhat battered chimney sweep, Hans-Christian Anderson "stove pipe" hat that I'd bought in a flea market. I had, in fact, arrived at the Embassy that morning wearing the latter.

Mrs. Stone, having learned of this sartorial mismatch through an alarmed Embassy grapevine, had called to say: "Bob .... I'm afraid you may have rented the wrong hat!"

But it was all okay. Coulda been worse: coulda come as the Giant Gorilla.

Farewell to Copenhagen; Farewell to the Foreign Service

As Midsummer of 1992 approached, we packed up Aunt Virginia's old piano and the rest of our things, said our farewells, and flew, with our dog Midnight and cats Sara and Tigress, back to the home in Arlington, Virginia, that we'd bought while in Trinidad. The girls made their transition from their Danish International School to those in Arlington. Gerhild began studies that would take her to a Master of Social Work degree and, eventually, a long-desired counseling career. I was sent to the State Department's "Retirement Seminar": the last of many, many training stints which I'd had courtesy of our taxpayers: training in Italian, Vietnamese, Norwegian and German; "area studies" prior to each new assignment, the 1980-81 Harvard year at the Kennedy School of Government, and, in 1989-90, the prestigious, absolutely superb nine-month long "Senior Seminar," the top executive training class of the Department of State.

I was a "free man" again — I could and did have political opinions; I could and did have bumper stickers on the car; I could and did get involved in some modest grassroots Democratic activism; I could and did claim that we deserved much better leadership than some that we had. I worked for a while with historian (and now National Archivist) Allen Weinstein at his Center for Democracy. And I wrote the treatment for what became a 12-part documentary on PBS narrated by Walter Cronkite. Called "Scandinavia!!!!!", it wouldn't have been unfair to deem it a shameless "infomercial": it eulogized much that had impressed and influenced me so much in the five Nordic countries ....and still does.

We had begun to save for the daughters' college educations from the time they were born. This, plus small inheritances from my grandfather, mother and aunt, invested in the "Clinton stock market" of the 1990's, got Julia through Virginia Tech and Anneke through East Carolina without loans to repay, and with credentials for the careers they're now pursuing. It also turned out that, with the mortgages on both the farm and the Arlington home paid for, my pension sufficed. This was true even after we split it, when Gerhild and I embarked on separate lives (but remained very committed parents). I moved full time to the mountain farm in Buffalo Gap which Christina and I had bought in 1975. This past December Gerhild, Julia, Anneke and I celebrated our 30th family Christmas together: this time in San Antonio at the home of Julia and her husband, Niamiah, then awaiting the arrival of baby Liam Charles, who made his entry on February 20, 2011.

Daddy had spent 30 years "fighting the Cold War." The Wall had fallen; in Europe much of East and West had merged; new and arguably more complex issues had come to the fore ...and serving as an American diplomat had surely become much more dangerous, in many more capitals, than through my career. But the Foreign Service continues to attract extraordinarily gifted men and women. And if they manage to keep some sense of humor, they'll do their country proud in spite of the crazies — both in Washington and abroad, and both within their Embassies and without.